Shirley Roberts.

Pat L. Christmas 1988.

A LIFE OF SONG

A Life of Song

Marjory Kennedy-Fraser

ANRO COMMUNICATIONS, CORTE MADERA, CALIFORNIA,

First printed by Oxford University Press 1929
Anro Communications has slightly updated the original text
and added the glossary, index and illustrations.

Library of Congress Cataloging-in-Publication Data

Kennedy-Fraser, Marjory, 1857–1930.
    A life of song.

    Reprint. Originally published: London : Oxford University
Press, 1929.
    Includes index.
    1. Kennedy-Fraser, Marjory, 1857–1930.   2. Ethno-
musicologists—Scotland—Biography.   I. Title.
ML423.K46A3   1987   780'.92'4 [B]   86–3309
ISBN 0–930623–02–9

Design: May Kramer-Muirhead and Malcolm E. Barker
Cover Art: Chris Riker
Typesetting: Publications Services of Marin
Type styles: English Times and Palatino
Printed by Thomson-Shore, Michigan

Printed in the United States of America

*"The world will end but love and music
will endure forever."*

Gaelic proverb from inscription on Majory Kennedy-Fraser's
commemorative burial stone, Iona Cathedral.

Contents

List of Illustrations ix

Foreword x

Preface 1

Geneology 2

Part 1. The Kennedys 3

  1. My Childhood 5

  2. My First Professional Tour 8

  3. The Kennedy Family 13

  4. To Australia 16

  5. In Melbourne 19

  6. Bush Travel 21

  7. New South Wales and Queensland 25

  8. Tasmania, South Australia, and New Zealand 28

  9. To California, U.S.A., and Canada 35

10. Concert Tours in the British Isles 39

11. The Cape 43

12. Italy 49

13. Italy *(continued)* 55

14. The Tragedy at Nice 62

15. Vocal Study in Paris. Gaelic Songs 66

16. Australia, New Zealand, and Canada Revisited.
     My Father's Death 71

Part II.   Life As Teacher 79

17. Marriage and Widowhood 81
18. Teacher in Edinburgh 84
19. I Lecture on the Art Song 89

Part III.   To the Hebrides 93

20. To the Hebrides. Eriskay and the Island Songs 95
21. First Hebridean Recitals. Eriskay a Second Time 105
22. Barra. Collecting on the East Coast 116
23. Collaboration with Kenneth Macleod 126

Part IV.   Fruition 135

24. My First Volume. London Recitals 137
25. Barra again. A Waulking. Benbecula.
     A Bridal Procession 141
26. Eigg 151
27. Visits to America 153
28. London Recitals. The Seal-woman Opera 157
29. The Lewes and Skye 160
30. The Seal Song 162
31. Conclusion 166

Glossary 173
Index 177

List of Illustrations

Marjory Kennedy-Fraser, age 18 4

The Kennedy family 4

Marjory Kennedy-Fraser and Alec Yule Fraser
on their wedding day 80

Patuffa's map of the Hebridean Isles 94

Patuffa Kennedy-Fraser 136

Marjory Kennedy-Fraser 136

Marjory Kennedy-Fraser; her last official portrait 171

Back cover: Portrait by John Duncan. Courtesy of the National
Galleries of Scotland.

Front cover: Drawing by Chris Riker

Foreword

Marjory Kennedy-Fraser was one of Edinburgh's most notable citizens. She was also one of the few exciting, original and entrepreneurial women that Scotland has ever produced. She won acclaim throughout the English-speaking world.

Historians have tended to overlook her, but we think that her autobiography, filled with incidents that are now history, will interest contemporary readers. We invite you to journey back in time with her through a Life of Song, of travel, and of interaction with well-known personalities of the Victorian age.

ANRO COMMUNICATIONS
Corte Madera, California. 1987.

Preface

This sketch of my life is an answer to many questions. Twenty years ago I began giving to the world the Songs of the Hebrides, the fruit of research work in the isles that lie off the north-west coast of Scotland. And this has brought forth such queries as: 'How did you first think of doing this work?'; 'What led to your undertaking this research?'; 'How did you begin?'; 'Where did you go?'; 'How did you proceed?'

Queries these that could not well be answered in one breath. The root of the answer indeed lies far back in the history of my Gaelic-speaking forbears, the Kennedys.

With myself, it goes back to my early girlhood, linked as it was with the career of my father, David Kennedy, the famous nineteenth-century singer of the Songs of Scotland. And I was not singular in this respect in the family, since my ten brothers and sisters, each and all, at one time or another, were associated with our father in his Life of Song.

Our family song-tradition goes still farther back, but this book must needs be confined to three generations: my father, myself, and my daughter Patuffa.

M. K–F.

6 CASTLE STREET, EDINBURGH.
        October, 1928.

Three generations of Marjory Kennedy-Fraser's family

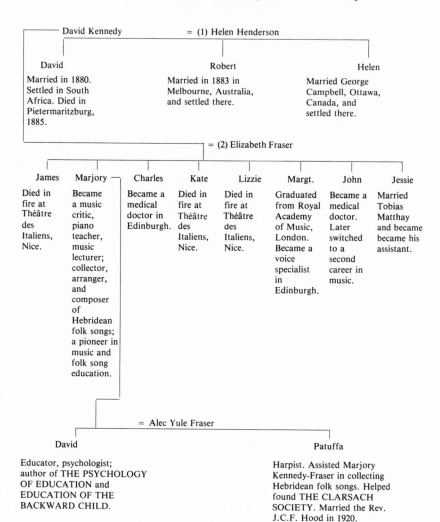

David Kennedy = (1) Helen Henderson

David
Married in 1880. Settled in South Africa. Died in Pietermaritzburg, 1885.

Robert
Married in 1883 in Melbourne, Australia, and settled there.

Helen
Married George Campbell, Ottawa, Canada, and settled there.

= (2) Elizabeth Fraser

James
Died in fire at Théâtre des Italiens, Nice.

Marjory
Became a music critic, piano teacher, music lecturer; collector, arranger, and composer of Hebridean folk songs; a pioneer in music and folk song education.

Charles
Became a medical doctor in Edinburgh.

Kate
Died in fire at Théâtre des Italiens, Nice.

Lizzie
Died in fire at Théâtre des Italiens, Nice.

Margt.
Graduated from Royal Academy of Music, London. Became a voice specialist in Edinburgh.

John
Became a medical doctor. Later switched to a second career in music.

Jessie
Married Tobias Matthay and became his assistant.

= Alec Yule Fraser

David
Educator, psychologist; author of THE PSYCHOLOGY OF EDUCATION and EDUCATION OF THE BACKWARD CHILD.

Patuffa
Harpist. Assisted Marjory Kennedy-Fraser in collecting Hebridean folk songs. Helped found THE CLARSACH SOCIETY. Married the Rev. J.C.F. Hood in 1920.

2

Part I

THE KENNEDYS

Left: Marjory Kennedy-Fraser, age 18. On tour in Canada. (Courtesy of Mrs. Marjory Piggott).

Below: The Kennedy Family

Back row (L. to R.) Helen, David, Robert, Kate, Charles. *Centre:* James, Elizabeth (their mother), David Kennedy, Sr., Jessie, Lizzie, Marjory. *Front row:* Margaret, John. (Courtesy of Mrs. Katrina Dawson).

1

My Childhood

The Kennedys in Scotland were a numerous and powerful clan in Galloway. But centuries ago a daughter of the ruling house there married a Cameron of Locheil and from the wild South-west took with her to the wild North-west a bodyguard of her own clan.

One day the Camerons came raiding to Rannochside. There was with them a Kennedy. A maiden who was tending a cow saw that he had taken the love of his heart for her—and she used her power. She asked him why this sudden descent of the Camerons. He replied that he might not tell her, but he might tell the cow, that she would not be there to-morrow morning! The maiden gave the alarm, the Camerons decamped without the cattle, the Kennedy married the maiden who tended the cow.

Of these were the Kennedys of Loch Tummel and Loch Rannoch and Loch Tay.

Our own forefather, John Kennedy, left Foss on Loch Tummel in 1745 to join the forces of Bonnie Prince Charlie, and returned in '46 a broken man. The Kennedys of Foss are scattered to the ends of the earth. All that remains of the *clachan,* where they dwelt, are the ruined walls peeping through a tangle of nettles and bracken.

Dreamers, singers, wanderers, they are still known, among the Gaelic-speaking Highlanders of Strath Tay, as the 'Singing Kennedys'.

After the '45[1], the Gaelic tongue, in which had been embedded the ideals of heroism and the chivalry of Celtic story, became a byword and a reproach, the Highland dress was proscribed, and the clans scattered.

Our folk came southward towards Perth city. The son of John Kennedy who fought at Culloden became miller of Ruthven, and his grandson, my own grandfather, was born in the city of Perth. So also was his son, my father David Kennedy, who became in time the famous singer of traditional Lowland Scots song.

Most of the mothers and grandmothers had been Gaels, but *his* mother, Catherine Taylor, was a Lowlander, born in Kinesswood, between Kinross and Leslie.

My own memory stretches back only to my grandfather, David Kennedy, born in 1800. To craft an independent handloom weaver, living in a self-contained house on the outskirts of the city, his loom in the lower story, he associated with this handicraft the serious study of music. A punctilious, superior, almost supercilious character, he was the leading precentor in Perth to a congregation of thousands, gave lessons in singing, and was known (for his serious theoretical studies) by the title of 'Auld Supertonic'.

My father was his only son. A greater contrast in character could hardly be conceived. David Kennedy the younger was a perfervid Scot. With an uncannily vivid imagination, a heart so full of sympathy that it responded to the sorrows and joys of old and young, in his middle and later life especially, he drew all men to him.

From his early days there had been a great stir of emigration among the Scots, and his dream had been to sing the songs of Scotland to the exiled Scots scattered through the world. But during the life of his first wife, Helen Henderson, he was unable to materialize his dream. She died after the birth of her third child, Helen, and only after his marriage to my mother,

[1]The Jacobite Rebellion of 1745.

6

Elizabeth Fraser, did he feel free to venture on the dreamt-of perilous career. At the age of thirty-two, with five children (of whom I was the fifth), he burnt his boats, left a prosperous business in his native city, and moved to Edinburgh. Here he gave himself up entirely to the profession of singer[1] and singing-teacher. My mother, as romantic and daring as himself, was eminently practical withal. She believed in him and in his dreams. After a year or two of intensive study and research in traditional Scots song and public trial thereof he appeared in London, and with such success that he gave in all a hundred recitals in town before setting off on provincial tours. Meanwhile we were all removed to London, where I spent my childhood between the years of five and eight (1862–6).

[1]He did meantime intensive study in voice production and interpretation, making frequent journeys to London for the purpose. When Sir Michael Costa learned that he intended to devote himself exclusively to Scots song he told him he was a fool.

2

My First Professional
Tour (1866-70)

At the end of three years my father felt that it was now time to try his fortune as a singer in the New World across the seas. During his concert-touring in Britain he had had at the piano Edward Land, one of the best accompanists of the day. But when it came to be a question of crossing the Atlantic, Land would not face the dangers and discomforts of such a voyage. My sister Helen was trained to take his place.

Kennedy's success on the other side was instantaneous and continuous. He did not return until he had sung all through Canada and the States as far afield even as San Francisco in the days before the opening of the Pacific Railway.

Before the departure for America, my mother had carried myself and three younger sisters—Kate, Lizzie, and Margaret —to Perth. There we were left with our grandmother. How happy I was in Perth! I had a schoolfellow who told me wonderful fairy tales and I took long walks into the country with my little sisters, where I preferred the ditches to the road because in them I found such wonderful wild flowers.

Of my own mother's mother I can just remember her standing at her cottage fire in the Carse o' Gowrie, making blackcurrant jam, the berries being from her own garden. As I see her, she is bending over the great jelly-pan with her back towards me. The image never turns that I may see her face. She was a notable character, Marjory Robertson. Born a century later she might have been a militant suffragette—had she lived a few centuries earlier she might have been burnt for a witch. So independent, that she argued even with the minister, yet so sympathetic and practical, that she sat up all night with the sick and went about her duties next day.

It was with our step-grandmother that we were left in Perth. Her husband, Robert Henderson, was a bookish man. From him I heard stories of King James I, the poet-king, so long a captive in England, cruelly massacred in the cellar of Blackfriars' Monastery in Perth by some of the Scots nobles. And I can still remember with what eerie feelings I would peer down through the gratings of the Monastery into the cellar where the poet-king died.

What a strong impression the removal from the noisy life of London to the quiet of the beautiful country round Perth made upon me! To this day, when I hear the queer hollow rattle of a leisurely, distant cart-wheel on a quiet country road, I am a child of eight, gathering wild flowers, the purple scabious, in the moist ditches, or walking with my two little sisters hand in hand. Or I am holding along the Tay in the gathering darkness towards the neighbouring village of Scone to the quaint prayer meetings that were held by old Mrs. Sandeman in her drawing-room, or I am dancing down the High Street, skipping with joy because I am learning to knit. And oh, the long hours of delight on summer days—are there any summer days to compare with those of Scotland's June?—on the North Inch, the green stretch of meadows by the river, where once a great crowd gathered and I saw a little woman in black (who, I was told, was Queen Victoria) unveiling a statue to her husband.

After a year in Perth, our mother came from America for a few weeks and carried us all to Edinburgh, where I began my musical education. Piano teaching in those days was a haphazard affair; and if I learnt rapidly 'it was mair by luck', I fear, 'than by gude guidance', as my master, I remember, occasionally read his *Scotsman* while I careered through my sonata. But he gave me good enough stuff to study, and I can look back at my own audacity when I asked him (as to the *Alberti* bass of many of the sonatas) why Mozart wrote such silly stuff. But I

9

must do him the justice to add that he initiated his pupils into the conventions of harmony, and that I got over the measles of dominant sevenths before I was ten.

Shortly after my twelfth birthday, our father and sister returned from America, and then began my apprenticeship as pianoforte accompanist. Every day my father sang with me for an hour, teaching me to read simple accompaniments at sight and to learn to anticipate what the singer was likely to do. It was no easy matter; he kept his renderings so fresh and non-stereotyped. Indeed, I had almost to imagine I was pronouncing the very words of the song with him on the piano keys before he was satisfied. In his readings of strophic song he used many of the devices that I later found familiar in Chopin—devices for varying in style the repetitions of a given melody. He used also a good deal of *tempo rubato,* which I recognized later in my vocal studies in Italy and, of course, in Chopin.

I played his accompaniments off and on for the next seventeen years, with years off for study abroad, and of all my varied artistic experiences, none has proved more valuable. His variety and definiteness of mood, the balanced *rubato,* the clear and expressive articulation, all of which he expected to be reflected exactly and immediately in the pianoforte accompaniment, kept me ever alert and furnished my brain with most of the needful technical devices of interpretation (alike as to shape and as to mood) that are called for in performance.

I made my first appearance on the concert platform with him in Lanark on 14 February 1870. The public held no terrors for me, going in on my father's hand. But I still recall the awesome effect of the handsome great dark bedroom in the hotel, with the enormously high, old-fashioned, four-poster bed, screened in all round with dark red damask curtains, the whole lit with only one candle.

Having made tentative appearances here and there with him, I was at last fully fledged in the summer of that year, when we made a long tour in the north of Scotland, beginning with Lerwick, in the Shetland Isles. He chaffingly told me then that he was prepared to accompany *me* for the first month, but after that he would expect me to accompany *him*.

Our hotel in Lerwick overhung the sea, and I can still recall the dreamy lap, lap, lapping of the water on the stones of the jetty, a lapping that crooned me to sleep at night and gently awakened me in the morning. The lapping water and the island glamour held me in their grip and I have never quite freed myself from them, although I have wandered on sun-baked continents the world over during many years of long and varied travel experience.

Shetland folk, although island folk like the Hebrideans, are mainly Norse, not Celtic, and there is no Gaelic spoken as in the Hebrides farther west, where my life-work later was to lie. In Lerwick I first saw women carrying burdens on their backs in long creels, knitting industriously the while at their famous fine woolwork, as they trotted along the stony pathways.

From Lerwick we sailed south to Kirkwall in the Orkneys, and here lived under the shadow of the old St. Magnus Cathedral. From Kirkwall, driving across the isle in the brilliant Orcadian sunlight, we heard of the mound-dwelling folk in the famous Maes Howe, and felt for the first time the strange allure of the Megalithic folk in the Standing Stones of Stennis.

Our tour carried us southward from Thurso to Wick, with its then stupendous fleets of brown-winged fishingboats, and thence by waggonette, for there was still no rail, to Dingwall. North of Dingwall there is one strong impression that remains. We were present at a great Gaelic open-air communion service, held in a wide curving natural amphitheatre of low hills. The congregation numbered many hundreds, most of whom had walked great distances to take part in the service. The old women, in beautiful white 'sow-backit mutches' (caps), wore great circular dark-blue hooded cloaks such as I was to see later worn in Belgium. When it chanced to rain, the big hoods were drawn over the delicate mutches. These 'hooded ones', as they came to be styled by the outside world, were at that time a great power in the religious life of the Highlands: they controlled the men, and also, through the men, the clergy. They have been summed up, those 'hooded ones', as a blend of the nun and the witch! Travelling to the communions from great distances, they walked most of the way barefoot carrying their footgear, which was donned only on their arrival at the place of convention.

From Dingwall we were able to continue the journey by rail to Inverness and thence to the Riviera of the North, the Moray Firth. It was at the aristocratic old town of Banff that we first heard of the outbreak of the Franco-Prussian War.

After this tour I was fully established as my father's accompanist.

3

The Kennedy Family   (1871)

We were in 1871 a family of eleven, the youngest two born while my mother was on tour in America. The family head-quarters were in the Grange, Edinburgh. James at the early age of 16 developed a good baritone voice, I was contralto, Helen soprano, David tenor.

After careful training by my father, and with the advantage of family blend of timbre and intimate, almost intuitive, common understanding and sympathy, we made an immediate success as concert singers on our first appearance in the Music Hall, Edinburgh, in the autumn of 1871. We carried on this *ensemble* work for nearly ten years. Our collaboration greatly lessened the burden of recital-giving on our father's part. He was still of course the supreme artist, we merely the relief. We were rather an extraordinary-looking quartet to be genuinely all of one family: David, 22, fair-skinned, dark-haired, fine-featured, looking no older than the baritone, James, only 16; Helen, of the same type as David, looking no older than I, although four years my senior.

From our home in the Grange we toured Scotland, returning as a rule for the week-end.

Scotland then was austere, and concerts in general and theatres in particular were looked upon askance. But our father was always a great favourite with the Scottish clergy. They fully approved of the Kennedy concerts and attended them gladly. There was then a very hospitable, but, for the guests, a somewhat uncomfortable fashion in the Scots manses of entertaining at breakfast. On a wet, dark, wintry morning, we would all have to turn out of our cosy hotel, leave the cheery coffee-room fire, and trudge along a muddy road to a manse breakfast where 'the minister' and our father held the floor while we young folk ate our eggs and drank our coffee in silence. I recall just such a morning in Kirriemuir, Barrie's 'Thrums'.

Ours was a very happy family life. We had great gatherings of friends at home on the Saturdays and went to the kirk in a body twice every Sunday. The minister came frequently to supper, and the children would be allowed before bedtime to entertain him, say with the photograph album, which was a great institution. Pointing to a photo of his father, John, a wee boy of four (he grew up to be a handsome man and a fine singer), remarked casually, 'That's a member of our family'. Margaret, aged eight, when asked at school what her father was, replied, 'A traveller.' 'But what does he travel for?' rather stumped her. However, at a hazard, she ventured, 'He travels for tea.'[1]

After two and a half years' touring the old country, plans were made for a round-the-world tour, beginning with Australia. Kennedy was then the most famous living Scots singer. There was no need for him to leave the comfortable highways of travel. But he believed in his vocation to carry the songs of Scotland round the world to all the Scots scattered abroad. So he travelled incessantly, fulfilling what he firmly believed to be his mission, and from this arose the need to envisage years of absence, the need to break up once more the home, the need to look forward to a long pilgrimage in the possible desert of hotel life.

And of all the sections into which my life naturally falls as I look back upon it, perhaps this long unbroken period of four and a half years' world-touring with father, mother, brothers,

[1]Later, when as a young girl she was doing her first colonial tour with her father, she heard a clergyman in Auckland, New Zealand, pray for 'the distinguished stranger that was in their midst'; and when she came home to the hotel she asked her father, at lunch, 'Who *was* the distinguished stranger the minister prayed for?'

and sister, moving continually over the surface of land and sea, looms largest. Unforgettable years, leaving their mark so deeply incised that I can still feel, while rattling along the pavements of Princes Street in the shelter of Edinburgh Castle or making my way down a no longer recognizable Regent Street in London, that my mind is looking out over vast spaces, leaving behind the familiar, and moving ever forward towards the unknown.

4

To Australia (1872)

It was during the years 1872–6 that this round-the-world tour was carried out. There had been in the previous twenty years a great spurt of emigration from Scotland. Australia and New Zealand, with their gold-fields and sheep farms, had attracted their share. A professional world tour in those days was not the easy matter of a few months that it is today. This was to be a long one. We sailed from Glasgow on 6 March 1872 in the sailing ship *Ben Ledi,* one of the then famous clipper ships whose record-breaking runs were as eagerly watched for in the press as are the ocean air-flights to-day. A 12,000-tonner to-day is not a very big ship. The *Ben Ledi* was only 1,200! A sailing voyage to Australia was then an adventure. There were auxiliary screw-steamers making the voyage, but my father, exhausted with the constant travel and unceasing public performance of the past ten years, had been recommended to take a sailing voyage as a nerve rest. We were bound, without a break, for Melbourne, a far-away port, not yet linked up with the rest of the world by cable.

Three months we sailed the seas without once touching land, through the tropics, becalmed in the doldrums, down into the roaring forties, keeping unnecessarily far southward towards the cold Antarctic in order to shorten the route and, if possible, succeed in breaking the record.

Day after day, week after week, month after month we sailed, our own family the only occupants of the saloon, with the captain and the first mate as table companions.

We carried our own little piano with us, a grand, specially cut down, for convenience in travel, to the Mozartian compass of four and a half octaves. Daily and assiduously we carried on our musical studies under our father. Our mother travelled with us, but took no part musically, save as a merciless critic.

When we were not practising or pacing the deck or watching the flying fish and the albatross or the lovely nautilus—the Portuguese men-o'-war—we were reading. A girl's education was supposed to come to an end in my childhood at fourteen. Grant Allen in advocating travel says somewhere that a young person's *schooling* should not be allowed to interfere with his *education!* Our father did not trust to travel alone. He kept us constantly supplied with books, and I remember on the *Ben Ledi* reading so steadily at Macaulay that I unconsciously imitated his style in the daily diary that recorded, Pepys-like, the daily menu, as well as the sighting of an island, the catching of a shark or albatross, the crossing of the line, the battened-down hatches in foul weather, and the enormous glens and hills of the sea, a sea on which our craft seemed no more than a leaf floating alternately on the heights and deeps of those living and moving sea-hills and glens.

In my diary a month out, I wrote: 'The three months seemed a long time to look forward to, now I look forward with regret that it will be over so soon.' But when we got down to the roaring forties it was a different story. There the seas were so terrific that our mate averred he had never seen bigger waves in all his seafaring experience.

How dull the sea would be but for its incessant movement! In the doldrums it is not attractive. The vessel goes 'drowsed as a snail loitering south'. South of the Cape it 'rolls till the brain is tired'. And we ran great risks, carrying too much canvas in the race for speed. In the effort to make good we several times well-nigh turned turtle, a sudden squall coming upon us with all our canvas spread. Such a rush then of hurrying feet, every man at the reefing. Never have I sensed such speed, save perhaps many years later when I was song-collecting in the little Isle of Eriskay in the Outer Hebrides, and a sudden change of wind and current made it possible at last, after long weary waiting, to leave the shore for the other side.

Among the passengers forward on the *Ben Ledi* there was a decent old Scots wifie, going out to Australia to join her son. She told us that one night, when the storm was terrible and we seemed likely to go to the bottom, she put on an entire change of clean underclothing that she might meet her Maker decently.

When the three months of sailing came to an end we sighted Port Philip in Victoria in the beginning of June. To the great disappointment of our Captain, who had run such risks, we were baffled at the very entrance to the port by unfavourable winds.

But when we arrived the moon was shining, the church bells on Queen's Cliff were ringing, a delicious smell of burning wood was coming to us from the shore. A little fishing-boat lay alongside of us—grateful sights and sounds and smells these to the wearied ocean-traveller. A barque that we had sighted off Cape Otway on our way in, passed us, after we had anchored, going ahead of us into the Bay, and we could hear from her decks the sailors aboard of her singing as they hauled on their ropes.

5

In Melbourne (1872)

Slowly next day we tacked up the Bay, arriving in Melbourne finally on 18 June 1872.

Young as the city was and far out of the world, it yet attracted good singers and actors from Europe, and there was a first-rate Italian Opera Company giving performances when we arrived. Our first evening in Melbourne, after dinner in the Menzies Hotel, was spent hearing *Lucrezia Borgia,* and later we heard Meyerbeer's *L'Africaine* and others of that ilk. Opera companies are at all times perilous financial ventures and this company was shortly to go on the rocks, but fortunately it left some of the members stranded in Australia, and these, in time, succeeded in establishing a school of Italian singing in Melbourne which later produced, from Scots-Australian stock, a Melba.

In Melbourne we fairly settled down to concert-giving and sang six nights a week for three months. So great was Kennedy's popularity, not with the Scots only but with the colonials of all types, that as he intended to travel into the interior he had at last to put a limit to this first Melbourne season. He was not allowed to depart from the city with his own farewell night. At a great special civic gathering he was presented with an illuminated address, and we young folks were each presented with a valuable souvenir. Mine, a necklace of cameos, lies in its case beside me, stamped in letters of gold:

A Melbourne Souvenir
MARJORY KENNEDY
1872

What days those were of sunshine and flowers! Flowers had been scarce in my childhood's days in Scotland, save in the month of July, when we got delicious tight wee posies of sweet-smelling country roses to carry with our white muslin frocks to the school examinations. In Melbourne there were flowers everywhere, roses and lilies galore, and we were often almost smothered in narcissus and geraniums on the platform after a Melbourne concert. In the queer Albert cars that were the cabs of Melbourne, we carried these home to our rooms.

We were the furore of the town, and appeared every night before crowded and enthusiastic audiences. People laid wagers as to our comparative ages, yet I was so shy, that when I walk again in imagination the steep streets of Melbourne, I find myself passing and repassing the door of a small draper's shop in Collins Street, in the effort to brace myself for the ordeal of going in to buy a pair of cuffs!

It was a very simple life. In the morning we practised both vocally and instrumentally. My sister Helen and I had to agree as to our hours of piano practice in the Concert Hall, and sometimes I have managed the unnecessary amount of eight hours a day.

Melbourne and its satellite suburbs, St. Kilda and the like, were surely then among the gayest, brightest spots on earth! And yet a young Presbyterian preacher, born in St. Kilda, Australia, coming to Scotland in the twentieth century and visiting his grandfather's native Isle, St. Kilda in the Hebrides (the Australian St. Kilda was colonized by Hebrideans), reported to me that, after a month spent on that lone Isle, the strongest impression he carried away was that of the intense happiness of its people.

6

Bush Travel (1872-3)

Australia was then still almost innocent of railways. From Melbourne we planned an eighteen months' driving tour through Victoria, New South Wales, and Queensland. To travel from Melbourne to Sydney one had either to go by sea, the easiest way, or by land—one cannot say by road, as roads there were none.

The bush, smelling like a chemist's shop, was totally unlike either the woods of Scotland or the backwoods of Canada. Gum-trees standing wide apart, the leaves long and thin, turning their edges to the sun, gave little shade; the earth, dry and hard, showed no mossy beds at the tree roots as in Scotland. Through this the bush track was seen ever winding its lonely way. Lonely, yes, except for an occasional swagsman or new chum making for up country.

The tracks were infested with bush-rangers. These desperate gangs held up travellers and made them disgorge, after the fashion of the old English forest outlaws. The Kelly gang, famous for murder and pillage, was finally caught on a road between Sydney and Melbourne, just a few days before our route took us over the same track. Kelly himself we saw later at close quarters, caged like a wild beast, behind bars in Pentonville gaol, a few miles out from Melbourne, and we thanked our stars we had not made his acquaintance earlier!

We were a large party to face bush travel. For ordinary travellers there were ramshackle Cobb's coaches carrying the mails, but these could never have accommodated our party. So my father bought a four-horse coach and buggy, and also saddle-horses which we mounted in turns, thus relieving the monotony of long days' driving. If we had a fifty-mile day, say, I rode twenty-five on our pony 'Jessie' and Helen the other twenty-five. If there happened a thunder-storm—which was not infrequent—I rode the whole way. But we had to learn to ride first, an experience I am not likely to forget. My first ride was on the sands at Warnambool. A long stretch of wet sand made a fine galloping course. My horse was being led by a Scot, famous in early Victorian politics, the Honourable James Munro, afterwards Premier. Accustomed to the easy security of the Colonial girl, from childhood in the saddle, he sent the horses off at the gallop. I landed on the sands between the horses, and I remember I could not lift my hand to my head, to brush my hair, for a fortnight. But when able to mount again, I became quite a decent rider. Many a thousand mile I rode, often leaping fallen trunks, most frequently with my father by my side, for he was a keen horseman, and we were great chums. A relief it was from the bumping of the coach, innocent of springs, over unmade tracks. We had an Irishman, Patrick Johnson, for driver, groom, and mentor, and he prescribed six miles an hour in the Australian bush and fifty miles a day, with one break for rest. When I was learning to ride, he remarked that my seat in the saddle reminded him of a new chum's bundle (swag), i.e. badly tied together.

The climate of Victoria, before the interior was opened up, was not ideal. There were frequent hot winds and dreaded dust-storms, when all windows and doors had to be kept shut. Occasional locust plagues, too, were to be feared. In 1873 they appeared simultaneously in Australia and in the United States, and we were caught by one while touring through Victoria. The plague had been devastating the country for several months. I was riding our pony 'Jessie' at the time. I have never felt any-thing like the stinging impact on face and hands, save, perhaps, years later, from a bitter-driving hailstorm in the summer of

1920 in the Isle of Lewis, when Lord Leverhulme put a car at our disposal there, to seek for songs.

Of snakes we luckily saw few. Kangaroos and the dark, thin, aborigines we came across frequently; and from a native woman, a *lubra,* I bought a baby opossum for a sixpence. Patrick made me a cage for it and I carried it about with me until it died in Sydney.

On the route from Melbourne to Sydney there were few towns, but where a halt had to be made, if a hall or barn even was available, we gave a concert. Our audience would arrive mainly on horseback, simply tethering their horses out to some fence for the two hours. 'Twa hoors at hame', my father called his miscellaneous Scots programme in the Colonies, and for the sake of those 'twa hoors' many a Scot has ridden wellnigh a hundred miles and back.

'At eight o'clock, as the shades of evening set in, the audience would begin to assemble. On all sides we could hear the soft thud of horses' hooves on the grass and the jolting rumble of carts. The room soon filled to over-crowding, folk were accommodated in the chimney, on the window-sills, and even on the roof, listening through the open skylights. . . At ten o'clock, the concert over, the audience would slowly melt away with cart-rumbles, hoof-falls, and phantom flittings as before.

'Ofttimes our own arrival at a lonely wayside inn would be a benighted one. From Albury on the confines of Victoria and New South Wales, we had a hard two days' journey to Wagga Wagga. With a start at five in the morning, in the grey dawning, our track wound monotonously through endless sheep-runs. At midday we pulled up at a creek and camped for a couple of hours. After tying the horses to the trees, we would fetch water from the creek, and, scraping together chips and twigs, make a blazing fire—the horses crunching their maize, the driver bedding up the fire and fanning it with his old slouched hat. When the "billy" comes to the boil he makes us tea and serves us with hot potatoes. . . A short siesta, then all is gathered up again, the pail and "billy" are hooked to the back of the coach and the monotonous driving figure-S winds again among the sparse trees. The day wears on to the darkening. All ears are on the alert for any sign of life ahead. We are making for Bilabong Creek. Suddenly a loud eerie shrieking laugh bursts out of the bush on our left. It is only the laugh of the jackass, which in quiet loneliness is echoed further and further off, until it dies in the distance. Again a long *trek* in silence, broken now only by the faint tinkle of a bell which, coming nearer, reveals a bullock dray and driver. We hear the cheerful news that Bilabong Creek is but three miles further. What was that? The barking of a dog, a light in the distance! At last the day's travel is over, only to find that there is no room for the party in the inn and that the male part at least must camp outside. But there, on the opposite side of the Creek, we see the friendly fire of some camping bullock-drivers. A shake-down within is found for our mother and sisters, and the others join the camping party by the fire. The short night passes in dreamless sleep; early next morning we are all again on the road.'[1]

We retained the coach and chaise and seven horses for eighteen months, doing Australia in this way, and I have often asked myself since why my father undertook this hard task.

It was a glorious experience. We were *en famille* like the Swiss Family Robinson and we were happy as the day was long. But my father was at the very zenith of his fame and could draw crowded houses in all the big cities of the British Empire, and need never have stirred from the easy-going rail and hotel travel of settled lands. He had a passion for seeing the world, no doubt, and the joy that he brought to the Scots abroad he got back in redoubled measure. In a letter to his father in Edinburgh, he wrote: 'I am happy, I have not headache nor heartache, nor reasonable wish that is not satisfied.' Our mother, too, was as passionately interested in travel and in song as he. Further, besides seeing the world, we all learned to rough it, to take everything as it came, and to endure to the end. To this day, when there is any travel on hand, I am ridiculously anxious to be ready in time.

'From my brother David's *Colonial Travel*.

24

7

New South Wales and Queensland (1873)

It took us six weeks' heavy constant travel to do the 500 miles between Melbourne and Sydney, but once there we had a good rest from travel. We sang every night in the city for ten weeks and enjoyed to the full the extraordinary beauty of Port Jackson and the surrounding country. We kept horses and vehicles, and many a delightful ride I had with my father round the famous harbour and into the environs. I can recall still the delicious fragrance of the pink-flowered shrubs that clothed the coast.[1]

In Sydney our brother Robert, a light tenor, joined us from Canada, and we were now a party of seven. From Sydney we sailed up to Brisbane, taking our horses and carriages with us. Our experience, driving and riding in the Queensland Forest, proved different from that of the bush in Victoria and New South Wales. Great forest trees, rich vegetation, mud axle-deep; thunder-storms—these are my memories of a four days' journey from Brisbane to the Gympie gold-fields. We made it a matter of pride, at all times, never to miss a concert date, whatever the obstacles. The unmade bush roads of Victoria had proved manageable, although at times maddeningly exasperating. But driving in Queensland through mud almost axle-deep to reach the goal at a given time seemed an attempt to achieve the impossible. Achieve it we did, however, and I rode in with my

[1] I recall, too, a famous sermon we heard in one of the Presbyterian kirks there, a long sermon, devoted to the question as to 'what kind of a fish it was *not* that swallowed Jonah.'

father to Gympie township at 7:30 p.m., mud from the hem of my long riding-skirt to the neck of its tight-fitting bodice, and yet was with him on the platform in a pink silk frock precisely at eight.

An element of sport in this? Well, yes, but it helped, for instance, to set the four-horse coach on its wheels again when it had overturned in the attempt to drive along the natural slope of a steep hill-side—it helped us to ride and drive on in the dark over unknown tracks, not by sight but by faith—it carried us across rivers that were ferryless and innocent of bridges—it helped me to sit tight on the box seat beside Johnson when one day, unexpectedly, with the four horses in full tilt, we drove down the sloping side of a gorge to find that at a sharp turn we had to traverse an improvised bridge thrown across a deep river, the bridge (?) consisting merely of two great trees thrown loosely across the chasm, the track between consisting merely of smaller saplings loosely laid and innocent of nail or fastening of any kind. Safety evidently lay only in speed and trust in the horses (especially the leaders) hitting the *exact* middle of the frail structure and so avoiding a one-sided tilting up of the loose saplings and the inevitable capsizing of coach and contents into the river far below. Horses are so sensitive that perhaps our feverish alertness was shared by them, for we (they) dashed up the other side at another hairpin bend and lived to tell the tale. My brother David, who was following on horseback, writing of the behaviour of the loose raft of saplings, said: 'As the coach jolted over it, the ends of the saplings came flying up, one after the other, like the hammers of a piano in a brilliant chromatic scale.'

Our farthest north in Queensland was Rockhampton. The heat here was fairly trying. Insects abounded, flying cockroaches and tarantulas. I did not sleep comfortably, I must confess, with a huge tarantula immediately over my bed.

But fruit also was abundant. A gardener (a German), who invited us to see his place a little way out of the town, when showing us round suddenly tore something up from the gravel path, and throwing it to a distance—it was a fine pine-apple—exclaimed, 'Dem veeds!'

Returning by steamer from Rockhampton we took on board a number of natives bound for an island *en route*. Their manner of disembarking was original. When the steamer neared the island they went behind one of the paddle-boxes for a moment to undress—it does not take long to remove a shirt! There were five men, the youngest a stripling of about ten years. Rolling up their bundles they tied them on their heads, then, gesticulating wildly and dancing on the slippery spars, they dived smoothly off into the glancing foam. One old man in addition to his shirt-bundle pushed before him a bag of flour.

> 'The long yellow beach to which they were bound shone in the slanting rays of sunset. It was thronged by other blacks, women carrying bundles of fishing-nets, men waving their arms and shouting to the swimmers. From out the thick groves we could see columns of smoke. Later, looking back, we saw five black heads still bobbing in the sea, then five dark figures emerging from the surf, then five swift runners scampering along the sand to join the excited groups of their own island folk.
>
> Back to New South Wales, we continued our road-travel. Here we encountered bush fires, the grass burning to the very edge of the road. Uno, our collie dog, had been with us all through. Many a weary mile he had wandered, but had enjoyed himself by the way—now dashing wickedly after sheep; now nosing a snake in a hollow log; now rushing after a drove of kangaroos; now sniffing a tree for a hidden opossum. One day splashed with mud; another powdered with white sand; another covered from head to tail in red loam; he showed traces of the country we had travelled through together.'[1]

Australian bush inns were sometimes pretty bad, but good and bad alike were inevitably left behind and there was always the open road and next day's adventure. At the end of eighteen months we sold our horses and took the steamer from Sydney to Tasmania.

[1] *David's Travels.*

8

Tasmania, South Australia, and New Zealand (1873-4)

Tasmania, erewhile the convict island, was now the delightful sanatorium and orchard of Australasia. Orchards, fields, and gardens stretched on every hand.

In Hobart, we were frequently the guests at supper of a gracious old lady, grand-daughter of Neil Gow, the famous Scots fiddler, and daughter of Nathaniel Gow, the composer of the tunes of 'Caller Herrin' and 'Bonnie Prince Charlie'. All Mrs. Packard's family were musical. One or two hours of music-making at her house were invariably followed by banquets fit for the gods, the table groaning under great heaped-up mounds of raspberries, gooseberries, currants, and strawberries with cream.

Our next port was Adelaide in South Australia. I recall great heat, sandy dust, demoniacal mosquitoes, and glorious grapes. These sold at three farthings a pound—luscious melting clusters. We lived on grapes in Adelaide—at night we could not sleep for mosquitoes.

After some weeks of Scots song recitals we gave a sacred oratorio concert on Good Friday. My father sang:

> 'Comfort ye, my people.'
> 'Every valley shall be exalted.'   *(Messiah.)*
> 'And God created man.'
> 'In native worth.'   *(Creation.)*

> 'Thy rebuke hath broken his heart.'   *(Passion Music.)*
> 'Behold, and see if there be any sorrow.'
> 'He was cut off out of the land of the living.'
> 'But thou didst not leave his soul in Hell.'   *(Messiah.)*

'Deeper and deeper still.'
'Waft her, Angels, to the skies.'   *(Jephthah.)*

It was a pity he could not have had two careers, one of them as an oratorio singer. His was no conventional oratorio manner, but a vividly conceived passionate interpretation of great themes, great emotions.

NEW ZEALAND

From South Australia with its heat and dust and mosquitoes and grapes we sailed for New Zealand, from port to port nearly 2,000 miles. 'Our first glimpse of New Zealand showed us a magnificent spectacle: sublime snow-clad scenery, lofty, sharp-pointed peaks towering inland.'[1]

Dunedin proved to be a very hive of Scots, and here we sang for over a month. Although midsummer, it rained much of the time. We found Dunedin an intellectually alive community and the particular bone of contention Butler's *Erewhon,* then just recently published. Butler was himself, for a time, a New Zealand sheep-farmer. We had to travel by roads here as in Australia, but as in Tasmania and South Australia we hired coach and horses, driver, and saddle-horses. The roads in the main were 'made', but the bridges were in most cases still lacking, and big was the toll of valuable human life that the unsafe fords yearly exacted.

Touring Otago, a delightful country, we stayed as guests one night in a Scots clergyman's house at Popotunoa, the concert being gifted by my father for the benefit of his kirk. 'The hall was the barn of a neighbouring sheep-farmer; the seats, planks laid on bags of grain; the gallery, the loft fitted with sacks of chaff. Folks arrived across the open country through long grass. Every shepherd brought his collie, the horses hitched up to railings, posts, wheels of drays. The barn was brilliantly lit with candles, which guttered out towards the end of the concert, and ran down on the folk below. When the audience dispersed, they

[1] *David's Travels.*

found to their dismay that their horses, alarmed either by the singing or the applause, had stampeded. "There's nine o' them gone, clean gone," said a man in a big flapping coat. It seemed a hopeless search under a black sky, the moonbeams striking through the rents in the clouds—strange shadows on the hills— the sound of the wind as it rustled in the high grass—the sight of the dark range far away where the horses were supposed to have strayed. . . Next morning we heard that they had quietly cantered home.'[1]

We drove for six weeks through Otago, a grassy country which reminded us very much of the Old Country save for its vegetation. 'The ever-present flax plant, a clump of green, drooping, sword-shaped leaves, on hill-side, river-side, road-side, became as monotonous as the gum-trees of Victoria. But as a set-off we saw battalions of wild Scots thistles pushing their purple heads between the tough green leaves.'[2]

There were many big rivers and at that time few bridges. The river Waitaki, dividing Otago from Canterbury, was much feared. We heard at Oamaru the unwelcome news that the Waitaki was up—it was reported barely fordable. Yet cross it we must with our four-horse coach, heavy luggage, small piano, and seven passengers. A fourteen-mile drive brought us to its banks; and here we waited three anxious hours, watching through a glass the opposite shore a mile off. A boat approaches. The head ferryman, looking for a safe ford, comes slowly across on horseback—a huge Norwegian with a long red beard. He orders my father, mother, Helen, and me into a boat with the luggage, a man wades up to his knees and shoves off our boat to the edge of a terrace, where, caught by the rush of the deeper stream, it floats round the end of a spit. Dragged then over a bed of shingle, the boat is finally rowed across a broad channel to the opposite shore. A more anxious matter still was the crossing of the coach. David, who sat on the box seat, relates how the big Norwegian, mounted on a bare-backed

'*David's Travels.*
[2]Ibid.

white horse, rode into the river and called on the coach to follow. The grey current rolled past.

'Crossing a bank of shingle, suddenly the leaders sank over their knees and the coach went down over its axles. Every now and then the vehicle lifted as if for an over-turn, those within gesticulating wildly. Another shingle-spit gained, they drove into the current at random. All at once the white horse sank to its belly and in a second the coach crashed to an equal depth, the solid mass of water moving past, not foaming but gliding swiftly. A few yards further, the Norwegian threw up the leading string, flung his hand back warningly, sank with an ominous plunge into an unknown depth, he and his horse being swept down the river. Clutching the bridle and hanging on to his horse's mane, he at last reached a point of land. Fortunately the horses in the coach stood quite still until he, dripping but hopeful, reached them again and by a sharp turn of the coach saved it from plunging likewise into the watery gulf.'[1]

But, if this land travel was dangerous, coast travel by sea was at times almost insupportable.

Having spent three weeks in dreamy Christchurch, with its quiet river and weeping willows, we turned our eyes toward the North Island with its rich vegetation, its volcanic wonders, its burning mountain, its geysers, hot lakes, and springs—in short, to Maoriland.

Wellington, surely one of the windiest of ports. The waters of the harbour, coming close up to our hotel, lapped its foundations as did the sea at my first hotel in Lerwick, and the wind 'blew as 'twere blawin' its last'. Only in the Outer Hebrides have I experienced a like anxiety when sailing was on hand.

The native Maoris we saw galore—tall, handsome, clever men; smaller, rather ugly women. By the shore a woman filling a basket with cockles—fifty years later I see our women in Barra at a like task.

Sailing up to Auckland, we pass Mount Egmont, one of the loveliest sights in New Zealand. A perfect cone, over 8,000 feet high, like a mirage, so lofty, so isolated.

From Auckland, our brothers were tempted to do a tour of

[1]*David's Travels.*

the then, for woman-kind, inaccessible Hot Lake district. Helen, Margaret, and I, with our father and mother, were to do it ten years later. But in 1874 only men were permitted, under Maori escort, to ride by bridle tracks to the far-famed pink and white terraces of Rotomahana.

Our mother left us at Auckland to take a journey literally round the world in order to see the younger ones left in Scotland. She travelled by California and across the Atlantic, returning by Suez. She thought nothing of doing this alone, and indeed took other lonely fellow-travelers under her wing.

Helen, my father, and I embarked from Auckland in a small coasting vessel to join the brothers at Napier. Oh, the horror of that trip! Five days in a miserable tub buffeted along the coast, at every unfavourable breeze running round some headland for shelter. We must have been specially disciplined thus early by Providence, I think, for the Hebridean Minch!

But the memory of it was such that when another was proposed, from Napier to Wanganui, we vowed (in the spirit of the Flying Dutchman) to do it by land, no matter what trials we might have to face. So early one morning we started a five days' overland journey. The road was not yet really open. There was much head-shaking as to our attempting it. But we had vividly in mind that last sea-trip. We *would* do this by land. Rain, mud, yellow lakes of mud, we had to plough through, day after day, until at last on the third day we came upon some superb New Zealand forest.

It was worth facing the perils and privations even of this drive to see the forest primeval. 'Tree-ferns, 20 to 30 feet high, reared their exquisite forms. Parasites of all kinds clung to and swung from the tall trunks of the giant trees. A stillness that was awesome was broken only by the dull rumble of our wheels over the dry roots, the harsh cry of a parrot, or the cooing of a pigeon. Swamp hens with red heads, purple bodies, wide-spreading tails, and long red legs stepped daintily about, paying little heed to the coach as it rolled towards them.'[1] But this passed, we neared

---

[1] *David's Travels.*

the really perilous part of our journey. At the Manawatu Gorge we had to give our hired coach *congé* and cross the mighty chasm, 750 feet wide, in primitive fashion. The bridge had yet to be built. No stone of it had yet been laid. Two hundred feet above the level of the river swung a wire rope, suspended from this a couple of planks. Man or woman, we had to get astride those planks and hold on like grim death while we were launched out over the abyss and perilously jerked across. Three or four days' rain had spoilt the smooth running of the pulleys. As my turn came to cross, the ropes overhead flapped aimlessly, until flapping against my defenceless hat they tossed it down into the foaming current below. Helpless, both hands holding on to the plank (which jumped about as if a spirit were in it), I could do nothing to save my head-gear. We were whirred onward down the rope which sagged in the centre and were then slowly jerked up on the other side. Worse even than crossing oneself was it to watch the wobbly crossing of each of the others in turn.

The chasm crossed, we had still the gorge to drive through. The narrow road cut in its precipitous banks was but in the making and no one could guarantee that a vehicle could be safely driven from end to end. This road-to-be skirted the gorge 300 feet above the river, a mere shelf in the rock only 18 inches wider than our coach. The drive tried our courage even more than the wire rope. Hundreds of feet above us towered the encircling heights, and round the windings of the gorge the road had to follow. At a corner, the man, who was green with nervousness, drove the horses out as if going into space, and just when their front hooves seemed to be slipping into the abyss, he dexterously wheeled the coach round. Only four and a half miles of it, thank Heaven!

Forty miles were added after this to our journey by reason of Maori disaffection, but at last, how welcome the sound of the waves breaking on the western shores, a sound which we had last heard on the east.

Coming south again at Christchurch, we were to sing one night at Port Lyttelton. The hotels at the Port were full. There was no train after the concert hour. There lay a mountain between us and our hotel in Christchurch. Our only resource, and one which we took, was an open railway trolley pushed by men through the tunnel.

It was now winter, and before leaving New Zealand we drove again through Otago. We recall still those exhilarating winter drives. 'The frost-bound roads, the congealed puddles, the fields white with rime, the light blue sky, the snow-powdered mountains reflected in clear lake and glassy flowering river.'[1] We never, said we, shall look upon its like again.

[1] *David's Travels.*

9

To California, U.S.A., and Canada (1875)

W e revisited Melbourne and Sydney and sailed in June 1875 for California. The route was via Auckland and Honolulu, and our vessel, a steamer of only 1,400 tons, was iniquitously overladen.

From Sydney we should have made Auckland in four or five days. 'But, a few days out, we met a terrible storm—the seas washed the decks day and night. On the sixth the storm reached its climax. Each billow rose as solid, unbroken, and dark as lead till its fluctuating ridge obscured the horizon—an image of irresistible power. Through the night the lightning flashed, the wind rose, a terrific towering sea broke over the vessel and submerged it from stem to stem. It had washed sheep and sheep-pens, pigs and pig-styes, hens and hen-coops clean overboard—stove in the wheelhouse, washed the boats adrift, broken into the captain's cabin—then smashed through the skylight of the saloon and poured into the engine-room, reaching within an inch of the fires.'[1]

We were washed out of the lower bunks, and my mother, Helen, and I had to climb into the upper, out of the sea that swamped the whole of the saloon and state-rooms. All male passengers were called to bale out. In a long line for hours they ladled out the surging waters with buckets, pots, pans, etc., their voices all but drowned by the noise of the water lashing up four or five feet on the walls of the saloon.

[1] *David's Travels*

Next day it cleared. Decks were strewn with a chaos of wreckage. For three days we had to look out from the woeful deck of our disabled hulk on sullen waters as we rolled helpless in the trough of the sea. On the ninth day we reached Auckland, where we had been given up for lost.

After repairs we set sail once more, now into the calmer seas of the Pacific. We had a memorable day off at Honolulu. Nothing surely can surpass the delight of suddenly, through great wastes of seas, coming upon a beautiful tropical island and spending a day there as irresponsibly as if one had dropped from Mars.

'The dark maidens of Honolulu with their bright-coloured flowing cotton gowns and wreaths of yellow immortelles on neck and hair; the great piles of gorgeously coloured fruit— mangoes, oranges, limes, plantains, and bananas; the Mexican ponies with their quaint lasso-horned saddles and leather-flapped stirrups; the superb Pali (or pass) to which we mounted in waggonettes drawn by a Kanaka; the view at the end of the drive—an abyss suddenly opening at our feet.'[1] Such are the vivid pictures of one day's eyeful of Honolulu.

The grey sea again, and in nine days San Francisco. The huge hotels, the Pullman sleeping-cars were new to us. We now travelled in fairly monotonous comfort, save that there were as yet no dining-cars and we had to eat a hurried meal at wayside stations *en route.*

Salt Lake City was a thrill, Mormonism was still strong, and we attended a service in the tabernacle where the men sat on one side, the women (in plain cotton sun-bonnets) on the other. 'A strange feeling crept over me on entering,' wrote David, 'a sense of worshipping in an unholy Pagan temple.'[2] A pleasant city, the streets lined with shady trees, while down each side ran full clear streams of water.

We sang here of course and had good audiences. Then on by

[1]*David's Travels.*
[2]Ibid.

Omaha and Chicago to Detroit, where, crossing to the Canadian frontier, we were once again under our own flag.

That autumn and winter and far into the next summer we toured Canada. As we sang in six towns per week and two Presbyterian churches on Sunday, I cannot record our doings in detail! We had enough of sleighing before all was done. Be it noted, the sleighs hireable for road travel then provided no shelter whatever, no wind-screens, none of the comforts of the most open motor-cars of to-day. They were merely lidless wooden boxes on runners.

One sleigh journey we are never likely to forget. It was from Listowel to Wingham, a stage of twenty-two miles. The thermometer stood 20° below zero; a fierce storm was raging. All house doors were shut. No one was out. 'The fast falling snow was drifing and all tracks were obliterated. The horses staggered and struggled through great mounds of powdery snow. We were in two sleighs which kept only about three yards apart and yet were continually losing sight of one another. We were driving in a white night. The cold was unspeakably bitter. The foam hung from the nostrils of the horses in long white icicles. Our coat-lapels were frozen hard and our cheeks glazed with scales of ice.' Charles (who had recently come out from Scotland to join us) had two blobs of ice on his eyes and he could not see till with difficulty they were picked off. David's nose got frost-bitten, also Charlie's cheek. The two had to rub each other with snow. When at last we reached a wayside inn they had to keep away from the fire (to which all the rest of us ran in an agony of cold), lest the nose and cheek should become running sores. Oh, the agony, the pain of such cold! One of our drivers vowed he would never go through the same again—'no, not for a hundred dollars'.[1]

We moved so rapidly and passed through so many different towns during that winter in Canada that when we wrote home, as we did every Sunday, it frequently happened that we had to

[1]*David's Travels.*

ask each other what was the name of the particular town in which we found ourselves at the moment!

The four and a half years' tour came near to an end in Halifax, Nova Scotia, in June 1876, and with a fortnight in St. John's, Newfoundland, we brought it to a close.

I cannot help smiling at my father's patient, persevering thoroughness in pursuit of his vocation. Newfoundland could only be visited by sacrificing to it a whole fortnight (the steamers called no oftener); yet with our minds straining to reach home after four and a half years in the wilderness of hotel life, we halted there—Burns's 'some place far abroad, where sailors gang to fish for cod'.

I was now eighteen years of age.

10

Concert Tours in the British Isles (1876-79)

Arrived once more in the mother country we returned to Edinburgh, whither our mother had preceded us to prepare the home. We made our head-quarters thenceforth in that beautiful city.

We rested that summer of 1876, a reunited family: father, mother, eleven sons and daughters, with sometimes our grandfather. The Kennedy grandfather had died while we were in New Zealand. The Fraser grandfather, when he came to stay with us in Edinburgh, evidently always regretted his garden in Perthshire with its berry bushes, and was not a little puzzled, I think, to understand his restless brood of singing grandchildren. We were fourteen round the table.

At home our brother David busied himself that summer writing up his notes of our travel. These appeared in book form as *Kennedy's Colonial Travel,* and were later followed at intervals by *Kennedy at the Cape* and *Kennedy in India.*

The original round-the-world concert party was held together until complete concert tours of the British Isles should be accomplished. These tours accounted mainly for the years 1876-8 and the winter of 1879. During these years we gave several seasons, with great success, in the large St. James's Hall, London.

Among our audience we always numbered John Forbes-Robertson, the famous London art critic (himself from Aberdeen), one of the keenest in appreciation of our father's art.

39

John Forbes-Robertson (whose son is now known as the famous retired actor, Sir Johnson Forbes-Robertson) writing to my father about Scots singers said:

When I come to John Wilson, I name the only man who has any real claims to be considered your fore-runner, or compared with you in any way. You are a born actor and possess a power of personation to which none of your predecessors could lay claim. In short, my half-century's experience and my own lyrical instinct entitle me to assert that . . . you are by far the most perfect and dramatic exponent of Scots song that Scotland has produced.

Our English winter tours took us to Manchester, Liverpool, and all the Midland towns. Dublin, Belfast, and the smaller Irish towns followed, generally in the spring, when the primroses and the larks made the world gay. In the English towns we remained as a rule a week at a time, and this freedom from travel afforded us ample time for musical studies. Indeed, when we severally spent years later doing intensive vocal study in Italy, we found that we could not do more there than we had managed to do while concert-touring in England.

While touring in Scotland we got home to Edinburgh for the week-ends; and as on a Saturday we had no concert engagements ourselves we young folks frequently sallied forth to concert or opera *eight* strong: David, Robert, Helen, James, Marjory, Charles, Kate, and Lizzie. All full grown, all young, all enthusiastic about singing. There were three younger, Margaret, John, and Jessie, also studying and listening intently to all that was said and sung by their elders.

My father when at home was wont to sit in the music-room surrounded by all the old collections of Scots song he possessed: the Scots Musical Museum; Herd's Collection; The Scottish Minstrel (really a collection edited anonymously by Lady Nairne a hundred years ago), and the collection on which he himself had worked in his early unknown days, viz. Chambers's 'Scots Songs Prior to Burns'. He was always adding something new to his repertoire, and among these there were rare characterizations such as 'The Weary Pund o' Tow' and 'The Auld Man's Mare's Dead'.

'The Auld Man's Mare's Dead' is to be found in the 'Songs of Scotland Prior to Burns', and is said to have been the composition of one Patie Birnie, who practised the art of a violer at the burgh of Kinghorn, in Fife, in the early part of the eighteenth century. With the song is given a portrait of the old violer, a portrait which, says Robert Chambers, 'exhibits a face mingling cleverness, drollery, roguery, and impudence in harmonious proportions'. Our father, while studying the song, kept the portrait of the quaint eighteenth-century fiddler before him until he was able to sing the song with the curious projecting lower lip of the original song-maker.

If the travelling in Scotland meant cold, raw, rail journeys in winter, these were always balanced by rare summer tours in the far North, when each day seemed to have some twenty-four hours of sunlight.

FRESH PLANS, 1879

By the spring of 1879 fresh plans for travel and study were made. There was no longer any desperate need to keep together the colonial group. There were now younger members of the family fitted to take their place. Lizzie, with a velvety soprano, had made a successful début in Edinburgh, and it was decided that she and I with the tenor brother, David, would suffice for a South African tour, travel at the Cape requiring, if it was to be at all swift, as light a load as possible. The choice in South African travel lay between the swift Cape cart and the slow bullock-waggon. We chose the former.

The reduction in the number of the actual concert party and the increase in the members available made it possible from this time onwards for two or three of the family to hive off and do post-graduate vocal studies, somewhere abroad, while the others toured.

Milan was still the centre of the professional singing world, and the names of the famous maestri, Lamperti, and San Giovanni were names to conjure with.

What a hotbed of discussion on voice-production was our

family circle in those days and for many years! Not only the professional singing brothers and sisters did their share, but the young medical student, Charles, brought his physiological and anatomical knowledge to bear upon the questions; and we all, with our father the most enthusiastic of the circle, lived and moved and had our being in the world of singing. And that world of singing is not merely a world of song. It is a world of great vocal possibilities, of great hopes, of great, sometimes desperate, disappointments. But those who once enter it may follow the will-o'-the-wisp of vocal resonance and the poise of the voice to the end of their days.[1] And who happier? Kenneth Macleod, in one of his lyrics to a Hebridean air, suggests this undying onwardness in 'Joy of seeking, joy of ne'er finding'. And so with singing. However long and unwearied the quest there is always a possible better than one's best.

---

[1] I remember one afternoon hearing Ben Davies, the tenor, attain for once the goal of his desire, a fine free resonant high note with a perfect blend, as we call it, of the registers. Margaret and I were sitting in the front seat of the balcony in the Usher Hall, Edinburgh. We turned and looked at each other: 'Got it this time,' we whispered. Our old friend, his accompanist (Harold Craxton), told us afterwards that these were the very words Davies himself used as he stepped off the platform.

11

The Cape (1879)

This year, 1879, was to see the family divided up into three sections: the medical student, Charles, sister Kate, and the three youngest with Helen, remaining in Edinburgh; while Robert and James, at the end of February, made straight for Italy; and our father, with David, Lizzie, and myself, undertook the tour of South Africa.

It was the year of the Zulu War. The British papers were full of it. On our arrival at the Cape, we found that we ourselves had brought the latest war news with us! Among our fellow passengers were a number of young Scots going out to the diamond fields in Kimberley, to try their fortune there. As yet no Johannesburg, all the adventurous world was attracted to the fields, where diamonds had been discovered only a few years earlier.

What a romantic spot Capetown was—Table Mountain, 4,000 ft. high, lying in a green crescent on the edge of the Bay, the villas and gardens creeping up its slope! Still an old Dutch town, the houses were square-roofed, windows deep-embrasured, the streets encumbered by *stoeps* projecting from each house, open runlets down the middle of the roads, which were lined with trees. And this peopled with a gaily coloured motley crowd: Dutch, British, Malays, Mozambiques, Indians, Natives, and 'Cape boys', the Malays sporting the gayest colours. The women wore coloured silk dresses in the sun—of blue silk or pink satin.

Three weeks we spent there, then sailed off to Port Elizabeth. As we bade good-bye to the towering, fascinating Table Mountain, clouds surged round its base, lapping up in great tongues or sunlit flames of mist.

A two days' sail took us to Port Elizabeth, where we were landed in surf-boats, because of the great sea swell. At night, the huge breakers were lit up by its phosphorescence, while nude natives, working at the unloading of lighters, staggered back and forth through the opalescent foam.

We were bound inland for the Orange Free State and Kimberly. There was rail only eighty-four miles eastward. So we bought a Cape cart, a kind of heavy two-wheeled gig—bought also the necessary four horses, engaging Saul, a 'Cape boy', as driver.

We had to travel, alas, with a minimum of luggage; and before leaving the coast I sat up till two one morning, deliberating as to what could be done without. There were the absolutely essential concert frocks. Beyond that I had to limit myself to one navy serge with an extra riding skirt, a suit that had to be brushed anew for all occasions and simply adorned with a clean tucker. Every ounce of luggage counted—even an opossum travelling rug, which we allowed ourselves, being adversely commented upon.

Driving in Australia with a heavily laden coach and four horses, we had been accustomed to go six miles an hour and unharness only once in the course of a thirty or forty miles' journey. But in the Cape, with a light gig and four horses, it was the custom to drive eight miles an hour, and outspan every twelve miles or so. And outspan Saul would, even with our inn in sight!

The veldt of South Africa we found as striking as the bush of Australia, but quite different. Grassy, untimbered, little of it under cultivation, wholly unfenced, it gave an impression of unlimited openness and expanse. Travelling for miles, we would not see a house nor meet a vehicle. A waggon drawn by eight or ten bullocks, raising a pillar of dust; a slow-flapping crow; a swift-darting *assvogel* (vulture) hovering over a dead ox— these alone broke the monotony of the veldt. But in hilly regions the vegetation was rich in lovely wild flowers and ferns and gorgeous creepers.

As in Australia years before, we had many heavy journeys. For instance (I quote from David):

> Leaving Fort Beaufort, at half-past six without breakfast, we travelled 14 miles in cold eager air to a wayside inn. Dense mist lay massed in the hollows. When the sun dispelled it, the heights flushed deep crimson, while the twigs of the mimosa thorns sparkled with rainbow-coloured dew. On the next stage, we passed the time practising our concerted pieces, the passing Native bullock-driver staying his massive bullock whip to listen astonished. Further, we had the famous Katberg mountain to climb—eight miles of steep ascent in mud, which we walked, while the four horses, hard breathing, dragged the cart to the 6,000 feet summit. Here we had to drive some miles in the fading light, dull purple mists beginning to shroud the deep-timbered *kloofs* that lay beneath us. Descending from our poetical elevation, we at last saw the welcome lights of our inn. . . The inns were primitive. The rooms floored with compressed cow-dung (much warmer and drier than earth), and washed with milk. The same stuff, dug out (like peat) from the cattle-kraals, was used as fuel.

But that night, to our joy, for it was bitterly cold, we had a blazing wood fire!

When we started next morning there was frost on the ground.

On *trek* we had to lunch, as in Australia, in the open, on tinned food and biscuits. Sending the haltered horses adrift, we lit a fire: no trees—we gathered twigs of thorns and set them alight in the lee of a big stone or in the scooped-out hollow of an ant-hill. Then on again to the inn where we were to spend the night. But if we arrived at mid-afternoon, no food was forthcoming until the Native servants returned in the evening from their own location, when the larders were reopened and food was served.

Once I remember arriving, soaked all of us to the skin, and finding no fire anywhere save one of dried cowdung, which showed only a single red spot of combustion about the size of a penny. No hope of drying our wet clothes and rug there. We had just to don them next morning and endure the dreadful damp until the strong African midday sun steamed it away.

Crossing the Orange River recalled New Zealand. When word came to us that the river was up, our father almost decided not to risk it. But he had trained up his children in the way they should go, and when *he* was old, they would not depart from it. I insisted that we should go on and keep our concert dates! So over we had to go. Lizzie and I and our father were taken across in a boat, two naked Kaffirs guiding it. At the crossing of the cart, the leaders reared and plunged and panic seized the wheelers. A man on horseback was got finally to guide the leaders across, the water sweeping into the cart at every lurch on the uneven channel. Crossing another river, we had again the good services of a native, who apologized for charging us what he considered the extortionate sum of 1*s.* 6*d.*, as the water was cold!

We saw great herds of springbok, the kangaroos of South Africa, and everywhere the dainty little meer-cat sitting on the ant-heaps with front paws uplifted, looking curiously at us as we passed.

Between Bloemfontein and Kimberley we came across a Dopper *Nachmaal* or Communion. They had made their encampment (waggons set in a square) in front of the inn, and fires blazed by each waggon and tent. There was no room for us in the inn, so we were accommodated in a tent with springbok rugs.

At night, the encampment with its fires and attendant bushmen was an arresting sight. Over the fires swung kettles, and a smell of cooking filled the air. Silhouetted against the red flare of the fires were the figures of the little bushmen, the smallest humans I have ever seen. Their fairy-tale, bird-like profiles gave an air of unreality to the scene, and one had an eerie feeling of having stepped, for a moment, into elf-land.

When we left at five the next morning, the tent-fires were still burning, and the Dopper-folk were going about their chores. At six that night we drove into Kimberley.

Kimberley, famous since for the emergence therefrom of Cecil Rhodes and his Scots henchman Dr. Jameson, was in 1879, still in its infancy. So new and unsettled, it was built entirely of corrugated iron. The two famous friends lived, like every one else, in a one-storied oblong of corrugated iron, the separate rooms simply partitioned off by unbleached calico.

Rhodes that year was absent from the fields on one of his periodical visits to Oxford as a student. Dr. Jameson only was at home. We were invited by him to dinner, and in spite of the primitive nature of the framework of the feast, dinner was served and host and guests alike dressed with all the formality of say Charlotte Square, Edinburgh. After dinner we made music in the partition that served as drawing-room! We little thought, at that time, that 'Dr. Jim', the most successful medical practitioner in South Africa, would become world-known later as the leader of the Jameson Raid.

We sang in Kimberley for two weeks to crammed houses, and found the audiences among the most responsive we have ever had. The 8,000 inhabitants of Kimberley at that time were not colonials. They had been only recently recruited from all over Europe.

The Kimberley mine was surely the biggest hole man ever dug, a vast crater alive with thousands of natives working like ants in an ant-hill.

While in Kimberley I enjoyed daily an early morning ride with some friends on a nice pony called 'Nelson'. When the time came for us to leave, we bought the pony and I rode her most of the way south again to the coast. Lizzie rode sometimes, but not being such an old stager as I, could not hold out so long. We had a group of *cavalieri serventi* seeing us off from Kimberley and they convoyed us about twenty miles south of the town. I might have married one of them—a good soul, a Scot, and a millionaire. I had no leanings that way. Indeed, it was remarkable how heart-whole we remained in our life of song and travel. 'Will they wed or will they wither?' wrote the newspaper poetaster in Melbourne in the 'seventies, and we only laughed heartily and passed on.

We were begged by the Kimberley folk to stay on and give them concerts, but we had dates—those dates that we always kept!

From Port Elizabeth we sailed to Natal. On arrival at Durban we were landed, because of the swell, in a huge basket, let down by a crane.

Durban felt decidedly tropical from Capetown, and I remember walking home after our concert there one night realizing the force of the Psalmist's words: 'The moon by night thee shall not smite.'

In Pietermaritzburg we came closely in touch with the Zulu War. The friendly Zulus, those who threw in their lot with the British, marched in one day to the town. It was an unforgettable sight. 'With a superb spring in their walk, their erect dark bodies decorated only with fringed girdles of wild cats' tails, carrying great hide shields and bundles of assegais, they moved rapidly along, singing a hoarse chant of victory.'[1]

From here began the homeward journey. At Capetown we gave a farewell concert to an immense audience. As we left, Table Mountain stood over us in its silent grandeur, bathed in superb sunshine.

[1] *David's Travels.*

12

Italy (1879)

While at the Cape we had received long letters from the brothers in Italy telling of their experiences in Milan; and it was decided that, after a short holiday in Scotland during the hottest months, they should return to Italy for further study and that I should go out with them. From their letters we learned that in the spring when they first went out they had taken up their quarters, after a long hunt for decent student digs, in a high flat near the Duomo. 'Imagine us', writes Robert, 'monarchs of a nice room looking out on a quiet street, enough friends here and lots elsewhere; enough money; health; and time to write a long letter! There, envy us until you hear how homesick we will be in a week!'

But homesick or not they were to stay and to work hard. The proposed six months of intensive Italian study lengthened out to over two years.

Daily they were at work from 7 a.m. until they knocked off at about 5:30 for dinner and the opera.

The brothers had been, so far, principally trained by their father. 'We can fully appreciate the lessons of the past', they wrote, 'now that the "doctors" of the profession acknowledge our state of advancement.'

Of the all-important matter of voice placing, a subject of universal discussion then and a veritable bone of contention in Milan, Robert wrote: 'Some "holoy" for a forward emission, some, more extreme, claim the nose as the proper spot to aim at—others again aim at a spot midway between the teeth and the tonsils and indicate the crown of the head as their true goal. Acquiring sufficient head voice is troublesome to a degree, and the low breathing with Lamperti is a matter so microscopic as to be almost invisible, but I think I have managed to grasp the "waistcoat pocket" breath which father has insisted upon so often.'

'The singers here', writes James, 'are very bad readers and, when attempting it, count audibly. One I knew counted invariably 1, 2, 3, as a sort of once, twice, thrice before taking the plunge!'

They took daily lessons in Italian with one Valenti, an operatic baritone, himself temporarily out of a job. As they intended making an appearance in opera they were interested in possible engagements or *scritture*.

The opera at the Scala was the highest rung of the music ladder in Milan. The stage there as large as the auditorium; the spectacle gorgeous; the orchestra, 140 players, mostly professors at the Conservatorium; the conductor working throughout without the score; the phrasing of the orchestra occasionally so daring in its balanced *rubato* as to cause the immense audience to rise to its feet and shout out its enthusiasm. (I have seen nothing like it save at a great British football match.)

At the smaller theatres such as the Carcano, the Dal Verme, or the Manzoni the audience was wont to be still more at their ease. Robert describes humorously a performance of *Norma* at the latter: 'almost everybody humming the airs and all with the air of thinking how much better they could do them than the artists.' 'At a performance of *Trovatore* the Azucena was a famous old singer, "La Galletti".' But even in her case, when for a moment she disappointed them by not singing a closing phrase well, there was not a hand and even a few hisses could be heard.'

The brothers, in preparing for an operatic début, had to lead a studious life. Italian (which they had been studying previously) they mastered fairly in a few months, their pronunciation coming easily to them as Scots, our vowels being more purely continental than those of the English. Their Italian coach, Valenti, took great interest in securing them a *scrittura* (contract), and after only four months' residence in Italy they made their début in the Opera House, Brescia. Only those who have faced it know how risky it is to attempt an operatic appearance as a foreigner in Italy.

An old impresario, Righini, when he heard that they had been studying Italian only two months was so favourably impressed that he engaged them as Edgardo and Enrico for a run of *Lucia di Lammermoor.* I remember how we laughed over the fact that they were obliged by Italian custom to wear flesh-coloured tights under kilts and that the kilts themselves were sometimes edged with lace. As for the Righini engagement of the two Scots, the Italians of his company naturally did not like it, and said: 'What the mischief do you mean by bringing two raw young beginners to sing the leading parts in this opera?' 'Raw beginners,' replied Righini, 'why, these *due scozzesi* have done more in two months than any other foreigners I have known do in two years.' And this in the Galleria[1] among a crowd of artists. But to their début. The old *impresario* gathered his company under his wing at five in the morning of the day of departure, and they all travelled sleepily from Milan. Arrived at their inn in Brescia, they made their way after breakfast to the theatre, only to find it occupied for the moment by another company. Delays followed.

At length the date for opening was fixed and the *prova generale* took place the night before. Of this Robert writes: 'There was the chorus, half a dozen wooden country-women and a round dozen of stalwart Italian bravoes, mostly singing tenor by some dispensation of Providence. All leaned on the prompter, an ex-chorus singer, always too late with his cues, coming in sometimes after the phrase was finished.' Of the final *prova,* James wrote: 'The curtain is down—orchestra tuning up— stage swarming with artists, chorus, supers. Old Righini rushing about in great excitement but evidently enjoying himself immensely. Valenti, Bob, and I promenade the stage. Valenti

[1] The Arcade in Milan, where most of the operatic contracts for the rest of the world were wont to be made.

gives me hints as to *scena* (action) for the hundredth time—one hand up, other hand down (semaphoring[1]?)—stand always three-quarters to the public; fold your hands high up on your chest, and so on.

'Then Righini hollers out to clear the stage—up goes the curtain—on go the chorus. I stump on with lance in hand (whoever heard of a Highlander using a lance!) and the *prova* is in full swing. When I have finished the first act Righini shakes hands heartily and congratulates me on my *scena* and all goes, both at the *prova* and at the first performance, merrily as a marriage bell.'

In accordance with an old Italian fashion, the morning after the début there was a serenade of six violins under the windows of the inn and a long speech was shouted up to the *Baritone egregissimo.*

At the second performance, he writes: 'I got more applause. After my first aria, there were some "Bravos"—I had to retire to the wings to lay aside my lance—then I was prepared to bow, but the applause had ceased. At the close there was very little applause, though I sang it really well. Still I didn't mind, but Valenti came running to me behind the scenes—Righini came— the conductor came—the Prima Donna came—all the chorus came—even the supers came, yes, and the wee humpty-backed theatrical tailor came and all asked me what I meant by insulting the public, not acknowledging their applause, and all prophesied I would get no more. I waited until they had all said their say, and then I retorted: "But that was a piece of the *scena* you never taught me—I shall know better next time".'

After James had appeared as Enrico, it was arranged that Robert should appear with him as Edgardo. Of the previous Edgardo, Robert wrote: 'The tenor was frequently out of tune, the *maestro* does not like him. But the poor devil has a wife and kids which deprives one of the desire to rival him—a wife who indulged in vigorous fits of prayer before a "Holy Mary" or a

[1]So this semaphoring was actually part of the sacred tradition of the Italian operatic stage.

Crucifix in her husband's dressing-room. And she didn't forget to hug him when he came off!' Preparing for his own début he wrote: 'We had an hour and a half last night on the stage in the twilight, when I went through the entire part of Edgardo much to our mutual satisfaction.' Describing the night of the actual performance he remarks that when Edgardo appears at the back of the stage, raised on two steps, upon which he lingers two or three bars, he has to descend slowly, with a deadly frown. 'When waiting for the cue, I stepped on at the right time, but it was some little while before I got on a proper frown.'[1]

Of Robert's début James wrote: 'The public were quite pleased with the first tenor, then why this other? Opposition helps to stiffen up some natures. The attempted hissing of the rival faction which greeted his first entrance merely helped to nerve him and he carried through the whole opera not only without slip or flaw but with a *scena* that astonished those who knew him best.' Jim, who managed to slip round to the front and hear the concluding scene from the gallery, writes: 'His death scene was dramatic . . . his tall, stately figure, his calmness, his lovely voice, the softest tones carrying to the furthest corners of the large theatre . . . his success was too much for Valenti, and when the rival tenor below tried to start some whistling, Valenti's fury knew no bounds—he leant over the front of the gallery and yelled at the ex-tenor "Ivideo porco" (envious pig) three or four times, and it took me all my strength to haul him away! Somehow I got him behind the scenes and he was positively frantic with feelings of delight at Bob's success, blended with rage at the tenor's contemptible tricks.'

Such was local Italian opera and its customs well-nigh fifty years ago. 'Still I envy our folk at the Cape,' wrote Jim. 'Italian

---

[1]Ellen Terry once confided to me that one of the chief difficulties in her stage experience had been the *timing* of the emotions, and she seemed to envy singers in that the music surely helped them in this. I was playing the little descriptive figure in my accompaniment to 'The Old Crone's Lilt', I remember, when she spoke of that. She bent over me and asked me to let her *see* me playing the musical figure, *slowly,* that she might analyse it and see how it was done.

opera will not run away with my affections. My heart's away in Kaffirland climbing that back-breaking mountain with the jaw-breaking name. Yes, there is a joy in a sing at the "Auld Scots Songs" at the end of a long toilsome journey successfully accomplished, that no amount of success in Italian opera can equal.'

13

Italy (continued)   (1879-80)

When we, the touring party, returned to Edinburgh from the Cape, we found our two Italian students reunited for a time with the home circle and all, as usual, enthusiastically pursuing vocal studies.

Our Fraser grandfather was with the family at the time, and it is recorded that he found the Italian vocal exercises 'awfu' dreich', but fiercely enjoyed Bob's singing of the malediction scene from *Lucia di Lammermoor*. There was evidently old Gaelic fighting blood in him still, although he had spent his life on the borders of the Lowlands.

An Indian tour meantime had been arranged for the autumn and winter of 1879-80 with David, Helen, and Lizzie as the supporting company.

Of this Indian tour, one of the most interesting experiences of the Kennedy touring life, I can say nothing personally, although I no doubt caught from my mother some of her blazing enthusiasm for the people of India, their country, and their art. But if I did not see India I experienced old Milan.

I shared my brothers' flat in the narrow street leading off the great Piazza, and daily our way across to the opposite side led us through the Duomo itself. They are going to 'ding down', I am told, all those typical old narrow streets in the centre of Milan with their courtyards and hammered iron gates and their glorious red roofs, because of the motors that hoot as they sweep tornado-like round the corners of the streets and hurry you into the immediate shelter of the nearest pend. The view of those red roofs and the white dream dome of the cathedral soaring above, seen from the balcony of a top flat in one of these old streets, is still one of the loveliest sights even of Italy itself.

But in 1879 there were no motors, and we welcomed the narrow streets for their shade in summer. It was early winter when I settled in with my brothers and was initiated into that unique old world of Italian singing. My brothers were now studying with Lamperti and San Giovanni.

I elected to work with an old ex-opera singer, Signora Gambardella, who in her girlhood in Bologna had studied with the famous composer Rossini. That he well knew the voice and its possibilities and limitations, his operas prove up to the hilt. His world of song was a world of *bel canto*. Old Gambardella, brought up in that world of beauty of tone, came daily to the flat, as was the old Italian fashion, and gave me a lesson of at least an hour and a half. She adored and detested me in turn. Lost in wonder at my musicianship[1]—I could actually transpose at the piano at sight, a rare accomplishment with the Italian singer apparently—she was equally horrified at my lack of appreciation of the kind of tone she wanted from me on certain notes. They all, the continental teachers, treated me as a soprano—I sang the 'Sonnambula' music with Gambardella—whereas I believe I was neither a soprano nor a contralto but rather a high tenor. Be that as it may, I got my score thrown at my head quite frequently, and once in her uncontrollable wrath the *maestra* tore a tortoise-shell comb out of my hair and threw it to the opposite wall. Ah, the singing students of to-day know not what we endured fifty years ago. But how earnest they were, those old Italian voice-producers! She lived by day and dreamt by night, I believe, on the problem of how to get that soprano voice of mine blended smoothly and perfectly with the lower voice, for she would have no breaks—she did not say, as

---

[1] We all scored, we Kennedys, in Italy, because we were good musicians, many Italians with good voices having to be coached in everything they did.

Mathilde Marchesi said to me later: 'As for registers and breaks, God made them.' No, she said: 'there are no breaks, no registers if you keep the approach always along the path of the head-voice.'

Most of the Kennedys, the sisters especially, had very difficult voices to manage. Margaret avers that she took fifteen years to unite her upper and lower notes, to attain to a smooth continuity of scale and perfect ease in the upper voice, *sotto voce,* but she arrived. Those who do not know anything of this physical vocal study are apt to regard the voice as entirely God-given, and the singer's art as a matter only of intonation, rhythm, phrasing; in short, of interpretation.

But all these things, although of the utmost importance in artistic vocal work, may yet be child's play to a musical, imaginative singer, whose voice nevertheless is physically almost unmanageable.

There are singers of course, most enviable, whose voice-production *is* natural—they know not how they sing—but not infrequently they lose their voices if they are put to any great strain. What may sound on the other hand like perfectly natural singing may nevertheless be the outcome of an intense and ever alert carefulness of production. Perfect technique ought at all times to *seem* natural. Conscious, carefully analysed articulation, for instance, must seem to the listener unaware of itself, no hint being given that the singer is carefully producing differentiated vowels and studied consonants. If any such impression be given it simply means that the technique is inadequate, faulty.

Dear old Gambardella, how shall I describe her? Rotund and fairly jolly, she dyed her grey hair raven black and arranged it in kiss-curls on a face that was too gorgeously made up. Her dress, always an ample skirt and short jacket, even if of black silk velvet and worn with diamonds. She snuffed, and carried on all occasions an enormous Paisley patterned handkerchief. Associated all her life with the world of opera or music-drama, she could conceive no other. Opera in Italy was the universal theme of conversation. The man in the street, the *cameriera* making our beds and sweeping our room would sing whole sections of the favourite opera being performed at the time. Any ordinary man you met spoke intelligently of the performance, and he would go no fewer than six times at least to hear a new work before he would consider that he was at all familiar with the music. There were practically no concerts. James sang, I remember, at one of the Conservatorium classical matinées 'O cessate di piagarmi' and other old Italian airs, but to an entirely select audience. The operas were little more than concert aria programmes held together by a thread of plot. But was this not somewhat better than the British 'grand' concert, not held together by any thread whatever?

Gambardella's voice-production teaching, over which she sweated and sometimes almost swore, inculcated the universally essential (1) open throat, (2) loose lower jaw, (3) tension at the nostrils (she screamed herself hoarse at times crying 'narigi, narigi'), (4) a heady emission *without any attack*—Marchesi on the other hand made a great point of the attack of the glottis, a dangerous practice possibly and one that the old Italians would have none of,—(5) and no choking oneself with breath. Daily she inculcated this ideal with a never-flagging enthusiasm, coming up the stairs of our upper flat always with the fresh hope of making me, Margherita, a singer after her own heart. A link she was with Rossini, with a world that was gone. But that old Milan of 1879 has also passed away. At the Scala we could then get seats easily in the highest tier of boxes for little over a *lira* (ten British pence), and we went every night when opera was on.

We took lessons in speaking from Ristori, brother of the famous Italian actress. He trained us in the art of speaking 'on the breath', akin to singing, save that the intonation is not, as in music, regulated stepwise after the fashion of crow's-foot gables, but is curved, like a thatched roof. To his training I owe the fact that I can still alternately sing and speak in public for two hours without fatigue.

As the winter wore on and I was steadily plodding on at my

studies, the brothers took engagements to sing here and there in opera.

James left us to reside in Venice, he being *scrittura'd* for opera there, where he appeared in *Poliuto*. He found Venice a miserable place in winter. Much of it, he wrote, was like a wet bedraggled Cowgate.[1] He remained there during the winter months, continuing his voice-placing studies with the Venetian, Pizzaloti, who found his voice *troppo cupo*—too closed; and 'now', writes Jim, 'he is opening it up . . . I open and open and open, but do not lose the "place". Sometimes I do—but I catch it again!'

Robert, in a letter to his father in India, relates how, at his sixty-fifth lesson from Lamperti, he quarrelled with the *maestro* and determined to go on his own way. But in time he repented and resumed the yoke.

When the Indian touring party returned in the spring, they came by Brindisi and Venice, and my father spent some time with us in Italy before returning to Scotland. He had studied the Italian method in his own early days, and the teaching of Lamperti in particular attracted him. His own production greatly pleased Lamperti, I remember—it was so 'open' without being 'white', and thus adapted itself to whatsoever 'colour' he wished to use on it. He was a very high tenor. I was his accompanist for fifteen years and know that he sang the Scots songs about a fourth higher than they are usually noted, but he could colour his voice so easily and articulate with it so perfectly, no matter what the pitch, that the public, if they thought of the matter at all, regarded him as a baritone.

While he was in Italy we all went to Lake Como and spent some time there together. It was probably the happiest time of his life, before the great tragedy came that gradually destroyed his native elasticity and undermined his health. It was certainly the crowning moment of the Kennedy family life. For wellnigh

[1] An old Edinburgh slum.

ten years some of us had been associated with him in the Songs of Scotland tours. Never again was the old team to appear together. David was to marry that year and leave for a settled position in South Africa, where he eventually died. This was the beginning of the disintegration of the group. On Lake Como, as at Milan, there were great discussions about voice-production, and two camps were formed within the family—the one enthusiastic Gambardella-ites, the other Lamperti-ites. James put it that Sims Reeves's art probably stood for the Lamperti ideal, Santley's for that of the Rossini-Gambardella.

My father was a Lamperti-ite. His own art was so subtle that, except to a critic like Forbes-Robertson, it was unrecognizable as such. Apart from the test of his tone, which was so pure and free that it could reflect the most delicate shades of feeling, he was a subtle artist in phrasing. He used the *rubato* with great freshness and effect. The freshness I can vouch for. Having been his accompanist for so long, I know that every time he sang a song I had to be very much on the alert in this respect. All the world is conscious of rhythm in music and poetry, although all the world may not be able to produce it. All the world can be hypnotized by it and can respond to the thrill of the 'return to the beat' of a great swinging *rubato,* a *rubato* which has swung them out to mid-stream and then landed them safely on the other shore. Just as the *rubato* of the Scala orchestra could make the audience rise to its feet, so the daring but perfectly balanced phrasing of a fine Scots tune can thrill any audience to enthusiasm.

When our father left us in Milan after giving a concert for the benefit of the kirk there, James went with him to Scotland. Helen remained with Robert and myself to take up study with Gambardella. Helen benefited enormously, her production having been a little 'tight' previously.

The early summer months in the city were very hot. But before the winter set in we had a delightful sojourn on Lake Como, at a little village, Carate-Laglio. We followed our *maestra* there and had our daily lesson as before. We had pleasant rooms looking out on the Lake from an old Italian residential villa, and we bathed daily from the stone terrace that led from the house to the stone steps from which we dived. As I fled along the flagstones in my bathing suit I could hear the remark, from the shady ground floor *salle,* 'Che belle gambe'.[1]

We made our own coffee in the mornings and boiled our eggs on a spirit-lamp; had our midday meal sent in from the little *Albergo* near—its main *plat* sometimes consisting of a myriad of little fishes; had a light cold collation in our room in the evening; and as the cool shades of night began to fall climbed the narrow stony paths that led upward from terrace to terrace to the steep sides of the hills that locked us into that world of lake and mountain. I remember reading Manzoni's *I Promessi Sposi* there with the same absorption that later I felt in reading Olive Schreiner's *South African Farm* in Cradock, South Africa, its natural environment.

We had for near neighbour at Carate-Laglio a retired famous ballerina who now, grey and old, was lady bountiful of the neighbourhood. We sat on her terrace, I remember, when one night a wonderful regatta of ships with coloured lights moved slowly up the lake, bringing with it the hypnotic strains of the music of the Scala orchestra.

We had a lake-side *padrona* who was quite puzzled by the fact that I could sit on her terrace reading the classical Italian poets, yet stumbled in my understanding of her own patois. I remember the like once in a country place in Scotland. I was a singer of Scots songs, and as all Scots knew their songs by ear it wasn't likely I could do anything else musically. My landlady set before me a book of hymns and asked me to play her one. I was puzzled. She was slyly trying to discover if I could read music! After a few months more of winter residence in Milan we returned to Scotland.

---

[1] 'Che belle gambe'—if legs had been as much in evidence in the eighteen-eighties as in the nineteen-twenties, mine had not called for comment.

14

The Tragedy at Nice (1881)

Thus in the spring of 1881 we set free James, Kate and Lizzie to go out to Italy. They were to work with Lamperti, but as he had left Milan for *villeggiatura* on the Riviera that spring, they had to join him in Nice. Six weeks later they were to have followed him to Stresa on Lago Maggiore. They arrived in Nice towards the end of the Carnival festivities, these being held later than usual owing to bad weather.

It was a miracle, Madame Lamperti said, that they got their heads under cover that carnival night. She recommended them, for permanent quarters, rooms two flats above her own. These they took and found themselves in clover. The flat was but two minutes from the Jardin Publique and the Promenade des Anglais, and just below were the Lamperti rooms, so they had merely to descend an inside stair for their lessons, which in old Italian fashion they took daily. Needless to say they enjoyed their surroundings. 'I wish you could all be here, Madge,' wrote Lizzie, 'the sky is deep blue, the sun bright, the sea glorious.'

Lamperti was specially a teacher of voice-production, and was so exacting as to tone quality and perfect evenness of the voice throughout that he was wont to aver that not the most famous public singer could pass through the ordeal of his critical listening.

Of their first lesson with the old *maestro* Kate writes: 'We'll have to keep our wits about us, for old "Lamp" mumbles' (he spoke always in the Milanese dialect), 'Madame bangs the piano and you don't know whether your head or your heels are upper-most, thinking of your breath, tongue, teeth, eyes, shoulders, front of head, back of head, or top of ditto!' They all three attended each lesson. 'The listening to the lesson', writes Lizzie, 'is almost as good as taking it—only the listeners think the singer such a duffer when he can't do what he's told.'

They were anxious to put in as much study as possible in the time, so they took lessons also from Repetto, Lamperti's accompanist. Repetto was very painstaking and his teaching was clear. One warning of his showed him at least a man of common sense—'the pupil must have the intelligence not to exaggerate what the master says'. Although James felt that he got more solid work done through Repetto, he adds: 'but at the Maestro's lesson you get the Lamperti *perfect ear* to bear on the results'.

The exquisite tone that Lamperti favoured James felt was almost too delicate for most public work. But he reassured him-self by the thought that if the natural course of public singing is apt to lead one into the wrong way, the more one knows of the right way the better. 'We study with all our mind and soul,' he wrote, 'and each day the road seems clearer.'[1]

'At Kate's last lesson', writes Lizzie, 'Lamperti was mightily pleased. Said she had made quite a *salto* (leap) and called her in Milanese a *brava tosa.*'

'One good lesson', writes Jim, 'makes Kate's heart bound with joy so much, that, if the next one is bad, she sinks immediately.'

They rarely walked on the Promenade at the fasionable hour. From 12 to 1 they had it very much to themselves. They had an old French landlady who went every morning to the market for fruit and vegetables, and sometimes Kate and Lizzie accom-panied her. She took a great fancy to them. She evidently was a romantic old dame, and 'Scot' spells romance on the Continent.

On the third (and last) Sunday, Lizzie wrote: 'Such a morning we've had of it! Oor auld wifie insisted on Kate and me going

[1]'Yesterday I got a valuable hint', he writes, 'as useful as "drinking in the breath": always in singing to think of the note you have left while aiming at the next.'

with her *au marché*. The auld body is very fond of oranges and loads us with them. This morning we treated ourselves to two wee bouquets of violets[1] and then walked with her all through the old town. We had quite a long chat with the auld wifie. She is awfu' fond of *Monsieur Jacques,* as she ca's our Jim.' The wifie was wont to sit and 'crack' with the young folks, as they drank their tea each evening. 'We've finished off two pots of jam already, mother,' writes Lizzie. 'Indeed, the auld wifie calls Kate and me *petites gourmandes,* especially Kate, for when Jim and I speak to her in French, Kate, she says, steals the jam and sups the cream. She brings us always *petits pains,* two each, so that one can't steal the other's share.' In her share of the correspondence Kate writes: 'We often take a stroll along the Promenade just before going to bed and we *do* sleep soundly, but we never (that is hardly ever) lie longer than half-past seven, when the old wifie comes and knocks us up. . . French lessons go well. Jim sails along splendidly, Liz speaks well too, but *me!*—though I have words and sentences in my head, it feels like jumping over a precipice or worse, taking a cold bath, to begin a French sentence.'

At the end of three weeks, on their last Sunday, 20 March, Jim writes: 'Weather here divine! Health never better—we all feel well and strong and hearty and fresh as paint. Early to rise, etc.'

As students, they naturally had attended the opera as often as possible. In Nice they had already heard, at the Théâtre des Italiens, La Donadio in Rossini's *Barbiere.* Lizzie, in her very last letter, wrote: 'La Donadio was here last week. We went *au paradis.* Donadio is really a wonderful singer. This week again she sings in *Lucia.* We shall go again.'

Three days later, on 23 March, James writes: *'To-night we go to hear La Donadio in "Lucia".'*

They wrote home as a rule only on Sundays. What moved him to write again on this day and to post his letter on the way

[1]Those bunches of violets, carefully dried and mounted, were sent to us later by the dear old dame.

64

to the theatre? That very night when they had taken their seats early at the Théâtres des Italiens, the house took fire. There was apparently a stampede for the exit, but they, alas, never reached it.

Robert, who was still in Milan, upon the first announcement of the catastrophe ran in the utmost agitation all over the city. No one had received precise intelligence. He wired and re-wired to Nice. At last, after some hours a dispatch arrived. It was from the *auld wifie* of their home letters, informing him that his brother and sisters had gone to the theatre, but had not returned. Sick at heart with fear and suspense, he abandoned negotiations regarding an important engagement to sing in opera in Naples and hurried to Nice.

In an agony of suspense, we others in Scotland awaited news. In the tremendous confusion caused by the catastrophe, Robert had difficulty in getting information. At last he wired to us: 'It must be told—they are all dead. The theatre blew up and fell in suddenly—death was instantaneous.

'Under the budding branches of the trees, encased in rude and cleanly coffins,' he wrote, 'I found them . . . Lizzie seems but to sleep and none of them have suffered bodily. There would be simply time for an acute mental pang and then all would be over.'

They were removed until burial to the vault of the English cemetery some miles out of Nice. 'At four o'clock to-day', Robert wired, 'I kissed them all for you, Mother, and nailed them down.' On the Monday they were buried, followed to the grave by many mourners. The whole town went into mourning.[1] The shops were closed, the Regatta and the close of the Mi-Carême were abandoned. A beautiful monument was erected to our young people, high up on the hill-side in the English cemetery, with the inscription:

'They were lovely and pleasant in their lives, and in their death they were not divided.'

---

[1]So many were lost in the fire. Lamperti alone lost nine of his students.

15

Vocal Study in Paris.
Gaelic Songs   (1882)

Following on the Nice tragedy, Robert gave up his Italian ambitions and rejoined us in Scotland. There, in time, we resumed our concert work.

This sudden loss was a staggering blow from which our father never recovered. Nevertheless, another twelve months' tour of Canada and the States was undertaken,[1] and was followed, on the part of Helen and myself, by renewed vocal study in Paris with Mathilde Marchesi, at that time probably the most celebrated *maestra del canto* in the world.

When I wrote from the States to arrange about lessons, I had an answer from her daughter Blanche fixing an interview with her mother. At this the famous *maestra* showed us a dried human larynx and explained the Garcia theory of the *coup de glotte,* and finally arranged that we should come every morning to her studio.

In Paris that summer we were again a party of three, Charles, the medical, now fully qualified, doing post-graduate work in the Paris clinics. Helen and myself were working with Marchesi, and we lived in a pension near to Marchesi's own *appartement.* Her studio, in which she resided, was then in the fashionable quarter, near the Parc Monceau, and there we were admitted

---

[1] Our youngest brother, John, accompanied us on this tour; and thus every one of David Kennedy's eleven sons and daughters had at one time or another taken part in his Scots song recitals.

every morning at nine. There was no fixed hour, as with Lamperti, for individual lessons. Her large, bare, deal-floored room contained only a grand piano, the necessary seating accommodation for the numerous students, and a glass-doored dwarf book-case containing bound copies of nearly all the music that she taught. Yet every student had to provide herself with two copies of her aria and lose no time in presenting one to the *maestra* as she sat at the piano and dispatched one singer after another, mostly with scathing sarcasm. We all believed that she enjoyed her own cruelty, although she vowed that she was harsh only that her pupils might learn to endure the greater harshness and indifference of the public.

Unlike the Italian singing-masters, she did not confine her study material to opera arias. She used plentifully the earlier Italian classics such as 'Tre giorni son che Nina', 'Ogni sabato avrete il lume acceso', etc., but although she was an Austrian (married to an Italian) she used hardly any of the fine German *Lieder*. The Hugo Wolf songs were not yet written, but she neglected the Schubert and Schumann and Brahmns. I remember one day a pupil bringing Jensen's 'Lehn' deine Wang' an meine Wang'' and her delight in it. It was new to her. Truly the operatic world and the *Lieder* world were oceans apart.

I had, long before this, fallen in love with Schubert's songs myself. Never shall I forget the day, in a stuffy little theatre in Queensland—I can still see the two classic female figures that adorned the proscenium and myself sitting at an upright piano down below in the auditorium—when I first came across the minor third followed unexpectedly by the major in the melody of Schubert's *Serenade*. It is an astounding melodic effect—and yet, when I heard Lloyd sing the song years after, I felt that he took it as all in the day's work!

Marchesi occasionally left her teaching-room when Gounod or his like called to see her, and in the afternoon an impresario might come to give an audition to a young artist, ready for the theatre. I was frequently present on such occasions. She gave us the run of the studio from 9 to 6, and I made full use of the privilege. She was famed for turning out *coloratura* singers, such as Ilma de Murska, and especially for their technique of the *note picchettate* order (i.e. hammered notes); and I remember one, a very clever *coloratura* singer, being so nervous before an audition that Marchesi, taking her by the shoulders where she stood on a little raised platform, shook her, in the end shaking her own fist at her. It takes courage to be a public singer. Indeed, Marchesi used to show her class a closed fist and say that a career lay in that. Her favourite sneer at any one who showed lack of courage was: 'You are fit only to marry.' I remember singing a love song to her, no doubt dolefully. She said, 'Is that how you take love in Scotland?' I have never forgotten its import. So pray, all who sing the 'Eriskay Love Lilt', put not dolefulness but great deep joy into the words: 'Sad am I without thee.' In those old Paris days I heard Blanche Marchesi sing once when her mother was out of the room, and she certainly proved her mother's maxim as to will-power, for she had no natural gift of voice whatever.

Mathilde Marchesi was an extraordinarily clever woman, had a vast knowledge of operatic tradition, had an enormous will power, could speak to her polyglot class in the language of each, and certainly tried to hammer them into capable artists. But I did not find her teaching sufficiently analytical to be of lasting value.

In her studio the piano, a long grand, stood parallel with the windows of her room—she sat at the keyboard end, the student stood at a music-desk at the tail-end. We all sat in lines parallel with the line of the windows. We could thus see as well as hear the singer who was under the fire of criticism. I watched eagerly, but never found that the teacher really explained in any clear way what was at fault when the tone was wrong, although we could quite well see from the lines of the singer's figure, for instance, that the breathing was bad when the tone was objected to as faulty. And the same with *rubato* phrasing. When fine, free, balanced phrasing was given by a naturally artistic singer, she would hold it up for admiration, but never helped us by analysis towards our attaining the like. Compared with the present-day teaching of a Matthay, alike in tone-production and in interpretation, it could hardly be called teaching at all. *'Sostenuto, sostenuto, legato, legato,'* wrote my brother Jim from Milan, 'the only use of learning singing in Italian is that it is a sustained *legato* language.' But a valuable discipline also is the perfect *sostenuto* of the double 'l' in Italian singing and the perfect *sustained silence* of the double 't'. I remember Marchesi being delighted with my own mastery of these points—she was rarely delighted with anything I or for that matter anybody else did! After achieving the normal in speech in song, how important it is, by the way, to realize the extraordinary possibilities in the way of expression that lie in slight (very slight) deviations from the normal in pronunciation, the slight *prolongation* for instance of a consonant. All true portraiture lies in subtle deviation from the normal, and song is always, is it not, portraiture of mood.

Quite apart from Marchesi's teaching, this experience in her Paris studio led in a way to a turning-point in my life. When I returned from her polyglot circle and rejoined our touring party in Scotland, I asked myself why I had never tried singing in my grandfather's tongue. For my maternal grandfather, Charles Fraser, had spoken only Gaelic in his youth. But he himself would not then be drawn—Gaelic had been so scoffed at in his early manhood: I had to look elsewhere for help.

We made a concert tour that summer in Scotland which included Oban and Inverness by the newly opened railway and the Caledonian Canal. In Grantown-on-Spey on the southward journey I found at last a man who could *read* the Gaelic, a *rara avis* in those days. Gaelic songs were being issued at the time by Mrs. Logan, Inverness, and from her publications I selected 'Gu ma slan a chi mi', 'Fear a bhata,' 'Mo nighean donn bhoidheach,' etc., and arranging them myself as unaccompanied trios for three equal voices sang them, with Helen and Margaret,

69

from that time forth literally round the world. My father fell in love with them[1] and backed me heartily in my efforts thus to introduce the Gaelic tongue on the concert platform. In Professor Blackie we found an enthusiast, in Mrs. Mary Mackellar, the Gaelic poetess, then settled in Edinburgh, an invaluable teacher. To her we went regularly for lessons, both in the language and in the songs. When we happened to be in Edinburgh we all three frequented her flat, and she gave us not only the pronunciation and meaning of the published songs I brought her, but added traditional songs and renderings from her own experience, renderings which we have ever since used. So even at that early stage, in 1882, I had begun to work in Gaelic song, on traditional lines.

[1]He had once himself sung in Gaelic, a translation.

70

16

Australia, New Zealand, and Canada Revisited. My Father's Death (1883-6)

In 1883-4 we revisited Australia and New Zealand. No romantic clipper-ship voyage this time, but a pleasant, smooth, luxurious trip by Gibraltar, Malta, Suez, Aden, and Ceylon, in the P & O ship *Carthage*. We found our brother Robert, who had preceded us, engaged to be married to an old friend, an Australian, and the wedding took place shortly after our arrival. There was little time for love-making in our touring life, and perhaps that accounts for our keeping together so long. My brother became virtually an Australian. A woman was supposed to take her husband's nationality, but is it not often the other way? Robert, anyhow, spent the most of the remainder of a long and honourable life as singer and teacher in Melbourne, and died there only a few years ago, in the fullness of his years.

On this visit we gave twelve consecutive concerts in Melbourne in the large Town Hall, singing only three nights a week, however. We were thus free to see and hear other artists. We were present at a big local farewell benefit concert given to the pianist, Max Vogrich, in the Town Hall. One of the artists taking part in the programme that afternoon was an Australian amateur, daughter of a Scotsman, Mr. Mitchell, one of the Scots who had come out to Melbourne some twenty years before and had flourished there.[1] His daughter, Mrs. Armstrong, we

[1]He and the Hon. James Munro and a number of other influential Scots got up a great ball in our honour in the Town Hall, and for once we danced our fill there instead of singing.

were told, was a fine singer. She sang that afternoon, how well I remember it, 'A fors' é lui' and 'Sempre libera degg' io' from *La Traviata*. As we came out of the hall, I remarked to Helen (who had studied with me in Italy), 'If that is an amateur, then all the professionals may hide their heads.' A few years later, having studied operatic roles with Marchesi in Paris, she astonished the world as Melba.

While in Melbourne my father missed the companionship of our mother very much. She had remained at home, not feeling well enough—she thought—to face the difficulties of long travel, even in its more luxurious modern form. He wrote to her, telling her how she was missed. She received the letter in Edinburgh on a Wednesday, she ascertained that a P.&O. vessel was leaving Southampton on the Friday. She cabled the name of the vessel, *Rome,* and sailed for Australia. She rejoined us in Sydney, which we revisited, by train this time, very comfortably, but equally unromatically, the romance recommencing, however, when we crossed the sea to New Zealand. They tell me now that New Zealand is much changed, that the primeval forest and the beautiful fern trees have been cut down, cleared. But travelling through it in 1884, we all agreed that we held it one of the loveliest of our colonies.

After a glorious welcome back, in all the chief towns, we spent a week of holiday travel in the North Island through the far-famed Hot Lake district of Rotomahana.

From the nearest rail, to reach Ohinemuto (from which travellers were wont to set out for the unique pink-and-white terraces, then one of the nine wonders of the world) we had a drive of over twelve hours. The road, a very bad one, over 50 miles, was newly opened. Ten years earlier, our brothers had done it on horseback, following a mere bridle-track 82 miles in length. With hearts elated they had set out, each with a pannikin and a coil of rope dangling from his saddle-bow, their guide cantering ahead and dragging after him the grey packhorse which wobbled along under tent-canvas, rugs, provisions, bags of oats, and tin cans. When night set in and the darkness became intense, they had been fain to throw their bridles down on the horses' necks and let the beasts scent out the track for themselves. For night quarters they had had to find shelter in the Maori huts, sharing the earthen floors round the fires with the folk, among them on one occasion a centenarian, a tattooed beldame. Two days from Cambridge saw them at Ohinemuto on Lake Rotorua.

Our *one* day's drive from Cambridge took us through some magnificent primeval forest, the Rotorua Bush—ten miles of it, we were told. But the road was so bad that it seemed more like twenty. The grand old forest trees, cut through by the road, towered so high that we had to crane our necks to see their tops. The undergrowth, which renders the forest impenetrable, was a riot of exquisite ferns, creepers, mosses, and lichens. I had always been a collector, and New Zealand ferns offered a grand field for exploiting my craze, so what was my delight when in this drive, we suddenly came upon a recently felled giant of the forest, to whose top still clung a glorious crest of the rare kidney fern. Fanatic fern-collector as I was, I bade the driver stop, leapt from the box seat, gathered a great clump of the fern (which grows only thus, far out of reach on the tree-tops), and returned triumphant.

As daylight failed and the moonlight struggled with the last rays of the setting sun, we began to feel anxious—even when the moon asserted herself and shone with intense brilliance—for the bush was so thick that we were at times almost in complete darkness. A mist rose, too, from the damp earth. Our horses spluttered and slid and stumbled, and our morphia'd driver (who had a queer tipsy drawl in his speech) muttered to himself. We were hungry and our feet were cold and damp. We had been twelve hours on the road. How much longer had we to endure? The horses broke into a trot, and down there—was that a lake? Yes! Rotorua at last and the village of Ohinemuto, and the entrance to the fairy wonderland of the famous Hot-lake District.

Next morning Helen, Margaret, and I rose early and went out. We found ourselves surrounded by fumaroles, bubbling mud, and simmering hot springs. There in a wee round hole a Maori woman was boiling a kettle. In a bigger hole, three or four Maoris were enjoying their morning bath, only heads and shoulders showing above the water. The Maori youngsters were vigorously swimming in the Lake itself—the grown-ups seemed to find the height of luxury sitting upright in a square hole full of hot water, and packed so closely that nothing was visible but a mass of heads and shoulders.

All morning we wandered between the Maori huts by pathways that were little more than a thin crust over boiling mud. The mud itself, in great pools, bubbled like porridge on either side. Now and then I was made aware, by the increasing heat round my ankles, that I was standing right over a fumarole or steam hole.

In the afternoon we all drove by Whakarewàrewa to Wairoa. It seemed the pathway to Hades—the whole but a section of the infernal regions broken loose. Sulphur fumes, terrific intermittent geysers, rumbled in the bowels of the earth, as if to give warning of their upward thrust. One, the most famous, sixty feet high, which had played when our boys had gone over the ground ten years before, resented evidently the coming of the *pakeha* (stranger), for it had taken the huff and had not played for years.

At Wairoa we were delayed. The first night there we felt a slight earthquake shock. Next day we attempted the lake Tarawéra, in an open boat with Maori rowers. But the day proved too stormy and we turned back. On the morning of the second day we decided to go on. My father proposed to stay behind, as he feared his weight might prove too much for the canoes which we should have to use later. But at 5 a.m. we all went down to the water's edge, father without his greatcoat intending merely to see us off. The Maoris went before, carrying our lunch, and Sophia, our half-caste guide, trotted alongside.

The lake was calm. We all, father included, got into the boat. Every one was in good humour. We girls (I quote from my own letters) sang Gaelic trios to the Maori boatmen. Father, who enjoyed dipping his fingers into the cool waters of the lake, suddenly remarked, 'The water is warm—it is getting hotter every minute'. We were approaching the hot creek that ran out of Rotomahana and we could already see the steam from the famous pink and white terraces rising over the top of a near hill. We had a tough bit of a walk from the boat. But mother was always to the front—she was a born traveller and no mistake. However, we reached the white terrace at last, crossed the hot lake in a canoe almost level with the water—and I couldn't help thinking it might feel uncomfortably hot if we had a spill. We bathed in the Pink Terrace. Sophia took charge of us, and we used the ti-tree scrub that accommodatingly flanked the great bare steps as a dressing-room. It was a cold winter's day. The water was deliciously warm. We came out and stood in the cold wind, our skin absolutely impervious to its chill breath.

Those strange waters had coated us over deliciously with a smooth siliceous deposit—we were gloriously enamelled—the sense of enjoyment was indescribable.

The terraced formation of the ground was common to all that country. But those two great twin enamelled terraces were unique. And in each terrace, as the waters descended (becoming cooler as they reached the lake's edge) they scooped out beautiful circular and shell-shaped pools, in which the water, even on a grey wintry day, was ever of a deep rich blue. I have never seen anything to equal the strangeness and beauty of this scene, save the colour of the shoaling seas on the sheen-white sands of our own Outer Hebrides.

Yes, New Zealand was surely a romantic country. At times, curiously enough, its water-ways get mixed up in my mind with those of our own Hebrides. We sailed so much by its shores, both of sea and lake, that I cannot say really whether the atmosphere I tried to convey in 'The Skye Fisher's Song', for instance, was a memory of my own mental state sailing up by Lake Wakatip to Queenstown in New Zealand; one of sailing from the Outer Isles of the Hebrides to the Isle of Skye; or one, again, sailing up the Cape Breton waters in Nova Scotia to

Badeck and Sydney. They all blend into a dreamy night-sailing and a late, late arrival on a quiet sea on which the reflected lights of the shore bear over a friendly welcome.

After this second and last Australian tour Robert left us, to settle permanently in his wife's country. We had now no brother to act as business manager and we did not care to introduce a stranger into the family group. Girls had not then invaded business premises; their place was still the home. So, when it fell to me to take up the necessary business side of the work (in addition to appearing still as singer and accompanist), there was some slight flutter in newspaper and printing offices and occasionally a look of dazed surprise when M. Kennedy, Esq. (a young girl) appeared to settle the accounts. *Mais nous avons changé tout cela.*

Since 1881 our father's health had been gradually failing. The shock of the Nice tragedy had radically undermined his strength. He still enjoyed his public work, however, when he set out for a farewell Canadian tour, with mother, Helen, Margaret, Jessie, and myself in the early summer of 1886. Jessie (now Mrs. Tobias Matthay), the youngest of the family, was then the latest recruit to the concert party. She had made her début in March of that year, in the St. James's Hall, London. So cordial had been her reception by the great audience, when announced by her father as not only the latest but the last of the Kennedys, that she might well have been embarrassed by the unceasing roll of applause that greeted her appearance.

With this quartet of maidens, then, our father set out once more for Canada and appeared in Halifax, Quebec, Montreal, and Toronto. The tour was to have included a visit to British Columbia. But all our plans were suddenly frustrated. He had been growing weaker day by day. His public talk was growing more and more impressive, and we all felt a shadow coming over us. How well I remember the last time he sang 'The Land o' the Leal'—it was so beautiful in tone and expression that it was with difficulty we went on with the remainder of the programme.

The disease, Canadian cholera, came on gradually; but he would not cancel his engagements, although we begged him to do so for his own sake. He had always gone on through everything: only twice during the twenty-five years of his professional career had he been unfit for work—once in India, when he was laid down with fever, and again in the north of Scotland, when he was confined to his room with a severe cold. On Tuesday, October 5th, we were to sing in Stratford, Ontario. We travelled from Sarnia in the afternoon. He lay down to rest. when he woke shortly before eight o'clock, he was too ill to move. We had to carry through the programme without him. We hoped it was but a temporary illness, but we had only a week of nursing. The windows were open all the time, for the Canadian autumn weather is lovely, and we looked out on the gorgeous foliage of the maple trees.

There was nothing gloomy about his death, nothing bitter about his memory. It was the peaceful end of a beautiful life. His wife and daughters were all round him when he died, and sang to him two verses of his favourite hymn:

> The sands of time are sinking;
> The dawn of heaven breaks;
> The summer morn I've sighed for,
> The fair, sweet morn awakes.

He was perfectly conscious, and moved his lips in unison with theirs, for he was too weak to do more. He did not die a stranger in a strange land. He was a man who loved much and was much loved in return. There were men there who had known him in boyhood and others who were friends of his manhood, and all proved most true friends. His remains were embalmed, and twelve hours after his death the funeral car moved to the station followed by hundreds of the citizens. We carried him home across the sea, and buried him where he had wished to rest, by a quiet wall in the Grange Cemetery, Edinburgh.

And thus came to an end a long and brimful chapter in the life of song of the Perthshire Kennedys.

Part II

LIFE AS TEACHER

Marjory Kennedy-Fraser and Alec Yule Fraser on their wedding day in Edinburgh. Spring 1887. (Courtesy of Mrs. Marjory Piggott).

17

Marriage and Widowhood
(1887-90)

My father's death in 1886 marked the end, for a time, of my concert-touring life. We might have continued it—my mother would have been pleased if it had been possible—but Helen and I had both been engaged for some time to be married, and public opinion was still apt to regard marriage as the end of a professional woman's career. I can still recall dear old Forbes-Robertson's dissentient voice in the matter. He held that we ought to carry on the torch that our father had lighted. But as Helen's fiancé was settled in Nova Scotia and mine was to be resident in Edinburgh, and we two were the more experienced of the group that remained, the proposal was not a practical one.

During that winter a movement was set on foot to erect a memorial in Edinburgh to the three famous Scots singers Wilson, Templeton, and Kennedy—a movement which materialized in a slab on the side of the rock on Calton Hill, close by the steps that lead up to the public path. In the centre is the portrait of my father, on either side that of the other two singers.

I remember singing in the Music Hall with Helen and Margaret at a concert that the Edinburgh musical world got up in connexion with this memorial. I remember it mainly because of an inexplicable feeling I had as of my father singing, not myself. I had been so long associated with him on the concert platform —possibly I could not extricate my mind from such association. My leisure that winter I devoted to writing a sketch of his career; and with it I incorporated a condensed version of David's travel papers, issuing the whole under the title of 'David Kennedy, the Scots Singer'. In that sketch I enter much more fully into details of my father's life than here.

My sister Helen was engaged to George Campbell, a successful Scot settled in Nova Scotia; I to my mother's young cousin, Alec Yule Fraser. My mother's father had been the eldest, Alec Fraser's father the youngest of a very large family. I had met Alec Fraser four years earlier in Aberdeen, in the early autumn of 1882. In the small ante-room off the artists' room of the Music Hall there, we three sisters were cloaking ourselves after the concert to walk the few yards down Union Street to our hotel. As I changed my shoes I heard a voice that strangely attracted me. I glanced through the chink of the door to identify the owner of the voice and saw a young man, my future husband, speaking to my mother. There are some who scoff at love at first sight, but undoubtedly for some of us there is such an experience, however little we may be prepared for it.

Alec Fraser was an Aberdeen graduate and was at that time on the staff of George Watson's College, Edinburgh. An Aberdeen fellow-student said of him recently that he was undoubtedly not only one of the most brilliant students of his time in Aberdeen but also one of the handsomest. He was a fearless scientist, a direct, uncompromising upholder of what he considered the truth—of him it might truly be said that he never shirked a fact, ignored a consequence, or feared a conclusion. At the time of our marriage, in the spring of 1887, he was science master in George Heriot's Hospital, one of the famous endowed schools in Edinburgh then in process of conversion into a technical college. Alec Fraser had himself there laid out and organized all the then quite new science curricula. It was an open secret that Aberdeen students were very hard workers, over-hard perhaps. My husband continued the practice of over-hard brain work into his professional life and at the same time undertook an immense amount of original planning and organization in connexion therewith. This gained for him at the very early age of 32 the head-mastership of Alan Glen's Technical

School, Glasgow, and thither we removed. But the air of Glasgow did not suit him. In a short time his health gave way, his lungs being affected. In search of dry air and sunshine we visited Cradock in South Africa (which I had visited ten years earlier with my father). He there seemed to regain his health, and returned to his duties in Glasgow. But he was not able to stand the climate and was shortly again ordered south. The return voyage to the Cape, however, was never taken. A week before the date at which he should have sailed, he died of pneumonia in my mother's house in Edinburgh. The date of his death underlined a strange fancy of his own in connexion with numbers. He had said to me that dates consisting of nines and multiples of nines were of peculiar significance in his life. He died on 9 November 1890.

We had two children, David and Patuffa, both born in Edinburgh. David was named after his grandfather, the famous singer. Of the origin of Patuffa's name I am often questioned. A Chicago journalist, to make a 'par', threw out the suggestion that it might be the Gaelic feminine of Patrick. It is Italian, however, Milanese. An Irish friend, daughter of an officer in India, a resident in Milan and a chum of mine in my student days there, paid me a visit in Edinburgh at the time of the little girl's birth. She it was, with the baby in her arms, who called her Madama Patuffa.

18

Teacher in Edinburgh   (1890)

With my two children, David and Patuffa, I remained with my mother in Edinburgh and took up there the teaching of singing and pianoforte.

After the Nice tragedy our mother could not agree to any of the younger members of the family going to the Continent to carry on vocal studies, so it happened that London was chosen as the place of further study for the remainder. Sir Alexander Mackenzie was at that time head of the Royal Academy of Music, and Scots students were highly thought of by him because, as he himself said, they had brains.

Margaret spent three years there and returned with the honorary degree, very seldom given to singers, of A.R.A.M. While there, in addition to her own full curriculum of studies, she acted as lecturer in Harmony. Her studies completed,[1] she settled in Edinburgh as a voice specialist.

With Margaret's return to Edinburgh, Jessie, the youngest of the six sisters—who had all in turn made professional vocal studies—was now able to leave home for further work. She too went as a student to the R.A.M. in London. For composition, she worked with Frederick Corder; and he thought so much of her work that he persuaded Tobias Matthay, the famous piano specialist, to take her as a pupil, although, being a singer, she

---

[1]Of course art-studies are never completed, and she has worked steadily ever since, finding great inspiration at times in Zur Mühlen's interpretations of the Art Song, especially in French and Russian.

was to make pianoforte only a *second* study. It was indeed great good fortune to be placed with such a teacher. He was then working out his now famous contribution to a reasoned science of the art of pianoforte playing and teaching. She was married to him in 1893, and made her home permanently in London.

I naturally saw a great deal of Matthay after my sister's marriage, visiting them frequently as I did in their country home in Surrey. His teaching attracted me enormously: it was so far ahead of anything I had come across in subtlety of analytical acumen. So subtly analytical and yet so constructively helpful, he led the way not only in the practical common sense of tone-production but also in the universally applicable common sense of musical interpretation in any medium whatsoever. His revelation of the laws of balance, of the structural manifestations of tone-sequence and tone-climax to be obtained only by a fierce economy of means, and how thus to economize and utilize these means, apply as directly to the lilting of a Hebridean lyric as to the performance of a symphony. Indeed, as a performer in any medium, if you have any real grasp of Matthay's Laws of Interpretation you can feel master of your means. You have got hold of the fundamental principles underlying all expression of the human mind in terms of musical tone. In short, the truth has made you free. For years before 1903, when his first book appeared, I was privileged to read his manuscripts as he toilsomely put into words what had never before been so thought out and expressed. I also read his proofs.

In early life, with my father, I had been familiarized with the practice of artistic interpretation: now, through Matthay, I was made free of the *laws underlying* the practice of the art. It took him quite ten years to prepare his first book, *The Act of Touch,* for the press, and many a summer holiday have I spent lying among the heather on the Scots hill-sides, helping with the revision of his proofs, or suggesting difficulties of comprehension that might be likely to arise on the part of the reader.

At last, in 1903, the book came out; and in the twenty-five years that have since elapsed it has revolutionized thought, not only in piano study but in all matters of musical tuition. In our own wide family experience of famous European teachers *(maestri)* of the technique and interpretation of music—and that has been an extraordinarily varied one—we have never known one who did, in a reasoned way, diagnose difficulties and faults and prescribe their cure as Matthay can. Indeed, with consummate teachers of style such as San Giovanni in Milan and Marchesi in Paris, teaching consisted mainly in the passing on, very vividly certainly, of traditional renderings. These the students were expected simply to lap up and reproduce. To be sure, on the physiological side, Marchesi showed us as a preliminary a dried human larynx. But, if one had any imagination, that leathery larynx was likely to suggest only tightness at the throat; whereas the old Italian teachers, to guard against such suggestion, were wont to say, contrariwise, the good singer *non ha gola*—has no throat!

Matthay unites in himself to an uncommon degree the scientist and the artist; and while keeping fresh in his mind the spontaneous flow of musical thought and expression he can yet put on the brake, so to speak, and mentally slowing down the process (as in a cinema) satisfy himself there and then as to what it is that makes the difference between the musically right and the musically wrong—a vast difference, but oftentimes depending (as in all art) on something so subtle as well-nigh to defy examination.

Matthay's life-work has put new heart into many a teacher and made their task a privilege. I sometimes look back on my own twenty years of teaching in Edinburgh and wonder now at its enthusiasm. What a waste of an artist's life it may be to teach students who are lacking in imagination, who take up studies lukewarmly, or (as often happened in Victorian days) as a sort of virtuous duty or even a penance! Yet one is certainly rewarded at times by a student who has long been groping in the dark and who, when given the light, almost falls down and worships the giver. Indeed, there are no finer friendships, I believe, than those between artist-teacher and artist-pupil.

One of the most valued friendships of my own life was that of Dr. Frederick Niecks, the biographer of Chopin who held the Chair of Music in Edinburgh University from 1891 to 1914. I had the privilege of being one of his students from the beginning of his professorship and of attending his weekly lectures for at least ten years—lectures on the History of Music, on Form, on Programme Music, etc., *sehr gründlich* lectures, in which he did not carelessly repeat himself but gave us ever fresh results of thorough study and research. Many a time when I called on him in his study in Dick Place—we were near neighbours in the Grange, Edinburgh—I could not find an unoccupied chair, they were all piled with the books he was consulting for his lectures. Thus his students—we were but few—without the eye-strain and fatigue of personal bookworming got the sense of proportion in history only possible by dint of long travelling down the road of history in successive centuries, even should much of the detail of the road be forgotten in the end. Our friendship, however, was not merely that of professor and student. We were close personal friends for many years.

In the summer vacations Margaret and I frequently made holiday tours on the Continent. Of course, we made the pilgrimage to Bayreuth to hear Wagner's *Parsifal,* which still in 1899 was not to be heard elsewhere. I always, in travelling, carry as little luggage as possible; nevertheless, I took that year a big score of *Parsifal* with me over to Belgium and down the Rhine. We were housed in Bayreuth in a quiet ground-floor room giving onto a lovely flower-garden; and we wandered up through trees in afternoon sunshine to the Festival House, where was gathered an interesting crowd of expectant music-lovers—dreamers, cranks too probably, but all apparently enthusiasts.

While on that tour we heard opera in many of the German towns, Munich included. Only here, on the borders of Italy, so to speak, did we find it thoroughly satisfactory, magnificent indeed. In other German towns, such as Leipzig or Frankfurt, the singing of *Italian* opera was very poor. Italian opera does not exist unless it is sung with beauty of tone and elasticity and *slancio*. In Germany it was often given entirely wanting in the grace and passion of the original. These cannot be found in a mere textual rendering from the notation, and perhaps are inseparable also from the original language. In Bayreuth, in the Wagner work, there was too much spitting and barking of the words on the part of the singers, and one wished for a heavier dose of the orchestra to cover it. Herr Balling, one of the Bayreuth conductors, admitted this, and said to me that the place to enjoy the Bayreuth performances was down below among the players. He even invited me to come there some time and sit among the instrumentalists, who would all be enjoying their work in their shirt-sleeves!

19

I Lecture on the Art Song
(1903-7)

In connexion with my preparation for the work I was finally to undertake in Hebridean song-research and recitals, I must go back to the 'eighties, while my husband was still alive.

In the autumn of '88 he had been attracted to the Summer Meeting founded in Edinburgh and carried through with great enthusiasm by Professor Patrick Geddes and Arthur Thompson (now Professor of Biology in Aberdeen). The members of this Summer Meeting studied biology and incidentally sociology, and in the evening held *ceilidhs,* as the Gaels would have called them—social and musical gatherings that followed each day's work. I frequently took part in the musical functions. After my husband's death I was asked professionally to conduct each year a series of lecture-recitals. One year it happened that my province was Celtic music. Of course, I had to look up and produce uncommon and typical examples of Irish, Cornish, Welsh, Manx, Breton, and Scottish song. For help, I wrote to my sister Mrs. Matthay, and she replied by sending me at once a copy (which she had borrowed from Mary Davies, the famous Welsh singer) of the then recently published collection of Breton airs arranged by Bourgault Ducoudray, Professor of Musical History in the Paris Conservatoire. This collection he had made, commissioned by the French Government, who had facilitated his work in every way, and had made provision even for the gathering into any given place of the best traditional singers of

the neighbourhood and the attendance therewith of an inter-
preter and Breton amanuensis to record the original words,
while Ducoudray himself noted the music. The French Government had done this at the instigation of a Breton professor, who
having heard Ducoudray lecture on Greek tonality, as illus-
trated by his song-collecting in the Isles of Greece, had said:
'Why not a like research in the Celtic music-lore of Brittany?'
This collection, set with a rare artistry and sympathy by Ducoudray, fascinated me. I felt that there might still be a like work to
do among the Scots Gaels, and that I could do it, if only I knew
where to begin. That was in 1895. But there were still ten years
to run before I should find the place and opportunity for the
work. Perhaps, indeed, I was not yet fully ready for the task
myself. Another phase of experience had probably still to be
gone through, essential, I believe, alike to the expert recognition
of the value and character of an air and to the artistic perception
of its possibilities. For so unaccustomed are we modern music-
lovers to melody minus harmonic interpretation that I have
myself known cases of total inability to sense melodic beauty as
such, without the support and formal suggestion of harmony.
My training in this respect came to me indirectly, through the
analysis of the Art Song.

In the Incorporated Society of Musicians, founded about this
time, I was elected a member of Council. Some of us got up lectures at the Monthly Meetings. I lectured occasionally on Songs
and Songwriters. In 1900 a few of us, including Professor
Niecks, felt that further opportunities of lecturing to young
musicians were needed, so we founded the Edinburgh Musical
Education Society, the first of its kind, I believe, in Britain. We
met fortnightly. We were expected to discuss questions relating
solely to matters of value to young teachers and to bring to their
notice books bearing on the subject they were teaching. This
was before there were such journals as the *Music Student* or
Music Teacher. It was our aim to give *résumés* of new books
and to introduce new composers. I had taken up the study of the
songs of Richard Strauss (a much-talked-of new composer

then), as helping to an understanding of his longer vocal and instrumental works, the text that inspired the song being taken as a guide to the composer's manner of thinking and expressing himself in music.[1] Niecks did not think this paper suitable for the Education Society. So I gave it with vocal illustrations in public, and it proved so successful that I followed it up with a long series of lecture-recitals on Songs and Songwriters. These I was induced to give year after year in Edinburgh. I gave them monthly during each musical season until they came to an end in 1907, because I had then found my own particular field.

In the course of these lecture-recitals, which included the songs of Schubert, Schumann, Jensen, Cornelius, Brahms, Tchaikovsky, Grieg, Hugo Wolf, etc., I analysed the musical means, separating the vocal from the instrumental, and used the drift of the poems to prove incontestably that composers meant definitely in their compositions the expression of a given mood and were not merely concerned with the invention of beautiful designs in sound. Hugo Wolf and Schubert we took up frequently, and these I contrasted and compared. For the vocal illustrations of the lectures—I played the accompaniments myself—I relied very much on the Kennedys, my brothers Charles and John and my sister Margaret. Baritones both, Charles and John were enthusiasts in song. They always looked to me to study with them the classics, Schubert in particular, or to read with them unfamiliar new music. Indeed, so keen were they that when they happened to arrive together in my music-room it was a case of rival claims as to who should sing first. For the lecture-recitals I also occasionally engaged local professional singers and coached them in their work.

These lecture-recitals occupied the winters of 1903–7. In the latter year one of the afternoons was devoted to 'A Visit to Bayreuth and Wagner's *Parsifal*', another to 'A Visit to the Outer Hebrides and Celtic Music'.

[1]Compare, for instance, Strauss's long dissonant introduction to *Electra* and the wandering dissonances of two out of the three pages of his little song 'Wer lieben will muss leiden', and one gasps at once his method in both, viz. simple consonance used with electrifying effect *after* a perfect inferno of dissonance.

This latter aroused such interest that I felt justified in confining myself in the future to Hebridean research and song. It was in February 1907 that I gave these first recitals; but for the story of the research work in the Isles and all that led to it I must go back to 1905 and earlier.

Part III

TO THE HEBRIDES

Patuffa's map of the Hebridean Isles.

20

To the Hebrides. Eriskay and the Island Songs (1905)

In the Summer Meeting gatherings in the 'nineties I had met a young Scots painter, John Duncan, who had specialized in Celtic subjects and had gone out to Chicago University as a lecturer on Celtic Art. In 1903 he returned to Scotland fired with the ambition to master Gaelic and to steep himself in the atmosphere of Celticism. He knew that I had long dreamed of doing original research work in Celtic music. So in 1904, when through a fellow-painter he discovered, so to speak, the Isle of Eriskay, he instantly wrote to me thence that this was the place for my work and that come out there I must, and that speedily. I could not go out that year—I had other plans. But in 1905 I ventured. It was then rather a formidable decision. Any degree of comfort on the journey—or on arrival—was uncertain. The certain discomfort went without saying. The island itself was a mystery and the getting away again a problem. But having been early inured to the hardships that beset the traveller ere railways and luxurious steamers opened up his way, I after a few misgivings—my son says I made up my mind about a dozen times to go and unmade it again as often—I at last faced it: so one night, in the beginning of August (I had been delayed because of working on a series of articles on Matthay's tone-production for the *Harmsworth Educator*), I dressed in what comfortable warm old clothing I could lay my hands on, taking with me only what I could carry in my hand, and left by the night train for Oban. I little thought, as I left by that night train from Edinburgh and got on board the little steamer sailing from Oban at six in the morning, that I was sailing into a world that would hold me in its grip for the rest of my life. Wet, sick, and weary—the Minch resents intruders—I stepped off the little steamer on to the Lochboisdale pier, where John Duncan and his friend Dr. Taylor were awaiting me. They hurried me, in a dreary drizzle of rain, into an open fishing-boat that was leaving at once for the Isle; and I shared with them the remainder of the lunch I had brought with me from home—Vienna roll and cream cheese, while the boatmen brought me some tea, bitter, strong, black!

We were landed about a mile from the house that was to receive us—the only modern house in the Isle, save those of the schoolmaster and the priest—and I was seated at supper by about 9 o'clock. I had hardly drawn breath when John Duncan brought me in a little girl, Mary McInnes, who sat on my knee and sang Island songs to me. In a little over twenty-four hours I had sailed, I felt, out of the twentieth century back at least into the 1600's.

Of all my varied experiences by sea or land none ever thrilled me as did this Eriskay one. I had been fairly silent and self-contained all my life, but just mention Eriskay to me and you touch a button that sets my talking mechanism a-going, and it does not cease until it is fairly run down. My son believes in securing a comfortable chair until it has exhausted itself.

It was certainly necessary, for the song-research I proposed to do, to go beyond the reach of the tourist steamer, beyond that even of the small local plying vessels, and such a spot was found in this little Island of Eriskay, lying far out to the west of Oban, and less known to the outside world than the remote St. Kilda. It forms one of the outpost chain of islands known collectively as the Long Island, which includes (besides Eriskay) Mingulay, Barra, North and South Uist, Benbecula, the Lewes, and Harris, where the nice peat-reek smelling heather-and-'cnotal' coloured tweeds come from. Miss Goodrich Freer, one of the few earlier visitors to the island—she published her experiences in 1902 in her *Outer Isles*—says: 'Eriskay is a mere gull's nest, scarcely worth the name of an island, storm-beaten, wind-swept, tree-less, shelterless, rocky. Although the distance across to the nearest point of Uist is probably not much more than two miles, the crossing is one not to be undertaken lightly. Always difficult, sometimes dangerous, it is not infrequently impossible.'

On that memorable first night of my arrival we were landed a mile from the Rudha Ban, where stood the chapel, the priest's house, and the house where I was to be lodged. To reach it we had to tramp through damp grass in the rain in the gathering darkness. Making our way over slippery rocks, we at last struck a pathway (the only road in the island, and that but recently made), and here and there, as though dropped at random on the bare rock, or nestling into the hill-side, we came upon long, oval huts built of undressed stone, innocent of cement or lime, and thatched with bent grass and bracken, fastened by ropes of heather. Silent figures moved quietly about in the dim, fading light—now a man, now an old woman, now a dog—all with the characteristic quiet gait of the Western Highlander, giving a dreamy character to the whole picture: a dreaminess which did not vanish, I found, even in bright sunlight, for when I woke next morning and looked from my window out to the sea from the house on the rock, I seemed to be on an enchanted island. The shallow water round this curving coast—that very shallowness which favoured Prince Charlie's landing here in 1745, and his escape from the English man-o'-war sent to dog him on his way over from France—this shallow water reflects the most gorgeous colourings, and we had great masses of deep purple, shrill green, and soft shell-pink spread out between us and the horizon. It was like Keats's

> magic casements, opening on the foam
> Of perilous seas in faery lands forlorn.

Our house stood with its back to the sea, and from the door on the other side we commanded a good general view of the island, the hill in the middle bearing about the same proportion to the sloping shores that Arthur's Seat does to the King's Park in Edinburgh. In fact, surround the King's Park with cliffs and the sea and you have a sort of counterpart to Eriskay, except that in the island you have more of rock and less of soil than you have in the Park. It is a curious fact that the strongholds of the Celts are generally found amid such surroundings. In describing Brittany, Renan wrote: 'At every step the granite protrudes from a soil too scanty to cover it.' These words are exactly applicable to Eriskay. And on this rock, with a little sandy soil in its hollows and a peat bog in one part, five hundred souls were making a livelihood by fishing, keeping a cow, a pony perhaps, and a few hens, and by growing little unfenced patches of potatoes and grain—grain which I have seen harvested by handfuls, roots and all.

Looking down from our point of vantage, the life of the island unfolded itself after the fashion of a beehive with a glass top. No fences, no roads (with the exception of the footpath), no carts, no wheelbarrows even; burdens of all kinds were carried, exposed to the view of the interested onlooker, in creels on the backs of the people, or in panniers on the flanks of the Barra ponies. Sometimes the load would be seaweed for manure; or a particular kind of seaweed which they spread on the rocks out of reach of the sea till, sweetened by the rain and sun, it is fit to be used for bedding, and very good mattresses it makes. The peats, too, had to be carried in creels or in the horse-panniers, and heather had to be fetched from a distance as there was none on the island; so boats could be seen leaving in the early morning for South Uist to fetch bracken and heather for thatching; and, returning the same night, men and women could be seen with the laden creels, toiling up the slope with their burdens, and storing the stuff in byres, against the needful re-thatching of the cottage roof. At all hours of the day children and old wives and maidens were to be seen herding, for in an unfenced world everybody's cow was always getting into everybody else's corn, and at any hour an exciting chase might be seen, when some four-footed feeder got into forbidden pasture. Then the boats, with their graceful brown wings, were a feature of the Monday mornings, going out to the fishing, and again, on the Saturdays, returning. Occasionally a boat went round to Lochboisdale with barrels of fish or the like, and returned with stores; and although every morning Father Allan Macdonald held service in the little chapel on the hill, it was on Sunday mornings that the whole island turned out. Then a long procession of women, young and old, of bairns, and of great, dark, brawny men, might be seen winding up the hill, as Father Allan came out of his presbytery, and himself tolled the bell which called them to worship.

All the southern part of the Long Island is Roman Catholic, and with this conservative form of the Christian Church we find the old customs, the old tales, the old songs, and a certain beautiful gentility and undefinable manner among the people. Father Allan's name was known and revered by all who took an interest in Celtic folk-lore the world over; Father Allan, the gentle enthusiast, the kindly priest, the sympathetic pastor, and Celtic dreamer, who was cut off by influenza only a few short weeks after our memorable first visit to his island. But his spirit still lives and moves among his people, and I felt his presence as much on my second visit as on my first.

Our nearest neighbours on the hill were Father Allan and his housekeeper on the one side, and the dwellers in the post office on the other. The post office was a little thatched cottage, which unlike the majority of the old 'Black' Houses could boast a chimney and a triple partition. Here I soon made the acquaintance of the courteous, well-informed postal official, Dugald Macmillan, and of his beautiful, dignified old sister, Mairi Mhor. Their little, clean, sanded kitchen, with its tiny home-made dresser, adorned with fine old painted bowls and jugs, its two wooden benches along the walls with accommodation below for peats, its barrel of flour topped with the baking-board (serving as a kitchen table), and its bag of oatmeal by the fire, was the recognized rendezvous of the island. There every one was welcomed to the evening *ceilidh*,[1] and when word would go round that we were going down there in the evening there would be gatherings of all who could sing or tell a story. The best singers on the island had remarkably low voices, and I understood that a low voice was particularly admired on the island, while high voices were preferred in Skye! One man, a young fisher, quiet in manner and dark and rather handsome in appearance, had songs that were not known to others, among these 'The Skye Fisher's Song' and 'The Mull Fisher's Love Song'. Each collector who takes up work of this kind has naturally his own melodic affinities; he gathers what appeals to him most, and the tonal idiosyncrasies of these airs recalled to me the character of some of the Breton airs in the unique collection made by Bourgault Ducoudray.[2]

One fine Monday morning I realized that a song of Gillespie's, 'The Skye Fisher', was not yet noted down. I intended leaving the island during the week, and I knew that he might go off to the fishing that day and not return till Saturday night. There was no time to be lost. I set out before breakfast to his mother's house, a long, oblong, old-fashioned hut standing back from the beach where Prince Charlie landed in 1745. A fairylike white beach it is, with sands that might have served for Prospero and Miranda, and where it is said Prince Charlie planted the creeping, fleshy-leaved, pink convolvulus which still grows there, and only there. Gillespie's mother came to the door when I knocked, and kindly bade me 'Thig a stigh'. I had enough Gaelic to know that I was asked to walk in. (I have had to acquire all the Gaelic I know, although my mother's father had no English when he was a boy, and my forebears on my father's side were also Gaelic-speaking.) She sat me down on a low, three-legged stool by the peat fire which was burning brightly on the floor, and seated herself on another. I had learnt by the experience of semi-suffocation to prefer those low stools to the high deal chair which was always politely brought from

[1]Pronounced *Kay-lee*.
[2]*Trente Mélodies* des Basse-Bretagne.

behind the partition for the stranger's use. On the low stool one was free from the smoke, which when it reached a certain height wandered at its own sweet will and escaped as best it might by the chinks in the 'dry-stane' walls or the crevices in the roof. The interior of the old hut was really beautiful in the morning light, which slanted down from the small deep-set windows on the dear old woman by the fire, who did not appear to regard my early visit as an intrusion, but cheerfully and promptly set herself to entertain me. She had no English, and I had little conversational Gaelic, so we sang Gaelic songs to one another; and she was pleased, and with Highland politeness said that I had 'Gaidhlig gu leor'. But by and by the old man came in, and he told me that Gillespie was already out in the boat, which was lying at anchor in the harbour, and that he would be mending nets till midday, when they were to set sail. This was getting serious. I wanted that tune. So I went to Father Allan with my tale of woe, and he listened with a glint of humour and sympathy in his eyes, and said 'Come with me'. I trotted by his side —he was a tall, spare man—down from the presbytery on the rock to the little harbour, and by the door of the small store— there was only one store in the place where you could sometimes get bread, but oftener couldn't for love or money—leant Dugald of the post office and the clerk who attended to the sales. Father Allan gave them orders to take me out in a small boat to the fishing-smack, where we would find Gillespie at his nets. The store was locked at once, the two men got a boat, and handing me off the slippery, seaweed-covered rocks in the low tide, rowed me out to the harbour. Gillespie was busy with his nets, and they chaffed him, I could see, about the strange lady who was running after him for his singing. So I had to wait about half an hour before he would be persuaded to sing, although the men urged him with 'Suas leis an oran'. He continued mending his brown nets in the glorious morning sunlight, with the purple sea lying quiet round us. But at last he yielded, and having once begun, sang verse after verse, and I got it noted down. He sang it with a peculiar woodwind-like quality of voice, which suggested a theme for orchestral treatment. The melody is most impressive when sung at a very low pitch. Indeed, the Islanders sing most of their songs at a much lower pitch than that at which I have transcribed them for ordinary use. They have quite abnormally low voices in some of the islands, and the city-dweller cannot hope to rival them in this respect.

Another of the frequenters of the post-office kitchen was Duncan Macinnes, a crofter-fisherman with a big family of bright blue-eyed boys who came to the *ceilidhs* in the wake of father or mother, and perched in twos on the corner of any available stool or vacant arm of a bench, drank in with evident avidity the songs and tales of their elders. Duncan had the 'gift', as the isle-folk put it, of story-telling and of song. He would repeat long *Sgeulachdan*[1] with a command of breath and rapidity and clearness of articulation that were the envy of all comers.

The songs were almost invariably long, consisting often of many verses strung on strongly characteristic recurrent refrains. They were intended, in the case of labour songs, to carry one over long stretches of monotonous labour. To this end it was essential that they should have an inherent circular quality; that they should tend to turn ever upon themselves; that they should appear to end not at the end but at the beginning; that the last note, contrary to custom, should in its very nature be unrestful and onward-driving, carrying the singer perforce to inevitable repetition. Indeed, the mysterious fascination of much of this music arises in all probability from this very quality of elusiveness which renders it so difficult to classify. The tunes haunt the mind's ear and endlessly repeat themselves, whirling ever wheel-like through the brain, since like the wind they come and go as they list, and have no hackneyed tonic by which we may hold them fast.

On this, my first visit to the Outer Isles, I could not give myself entirely to song-collecting, as I was still busy finishing

[1]Tales, pronounced *scale-ach-can*.

those promised articles on Matthay's pianoforte teachings for the *Harmsworth Educator*. I improvised a desk at my bedroom window of a rough deal provision case, standing it up on end, the lidless side yielding accommodation for the knees, the lid resting on top like the letter T. But the view from the window was so entrancing, the purples, blues, greens, and shell-pink of sea and shore so intoxicating, that it was impossible to keep my mind from straying. My companions told me I would get used to it in time.

In the evenings we went down to the cottages to *ceilidh*. In the old 'Black' House of John McInnes the social gathering was literally *round* the fire. It burned in the middle of the rock floor encircled alike by dogs and human guests. Other interested onlookers and listeners were the hens, who roosted in the rafters, but came down occasionally when anything unusual was afoot. And no doubt a most intrigued listener to the stories and songs was the weak-legged wee calf that occupied the far end of the *salle*.

On my first visit to the Isle we were a party of five, including Rachel Annand Taylor, one of the brilliant group of young poets hailing from Aberdeen University, where they had been inspired probably by Professor Grierson. The day after my arrival, and before she and her husband left the Island, we all five made an excursion towards the other end of the Isle, where there was a disused harbour, a long, enclosed, sheltered inlet of the sea. As we reached the smooth green turf overhanging its quiet waters, I felt so overcome by the eeriness of the spot that I knelt down on the mossy quay, and looking into the oily depths murmured, 'Pelleas and Melisande'. A look of mutual understanding passed from one to the other. They had brought me here on purpose to see if the place would affect me as it had affected them.

At the time of my first visit to the Isle there was only one weekly mail and no cable communication. So my folk began to think from my continued silence that I was lost to them altogether. That outgoing mail took away our letters in a wee open boat in the early morning, and after a trip across the sound and back again Dugald delivered to us the incoming mail. Thus it was impossible to answer our letters until a week had passed.

I left the Island one morning early, after having miserably waited morning after morning for a whole week for suitable weather—*possible* weather for the seamen be it understood, not merely suitable for me. I had to hold myself in readiness each morning before eight with my bag packed ready for travel. Hope deferred, certainly. But morning after morning word came to me that the men could not go out, the current rendering it impossible. When we did leave at last, in the little open boat, we had a rough passage. The last thing I noted as we drew away from the shore was the tall, spare figure of Father Allan (The Lord of the Isles, they called him) coming out from the door of his presbytery on the rock and crossing to the little chapel which commanded the harbour.

21

First Hebridean Recitals.
Eriskay a Second Time   (1907)

From Eriskay I had brought with me a good haul of unpublished melodies to add to the existing traditional music-lore of Scotland. But, returning to Edinburgh, I was again engulfed in my ordinary professional work. I was chief musical critic of the Edinburgh *Evening News* for ten years; all spare time left, after teaching from nine to four, had to be given to the preparation of the lecture-recitals, for which I had to do a good deal of reading, chiefly in German.

I had certainly brought home with me a good haul of tunes— others could collect and write down the Gaelic words. Father Allan was to send these after me. But alas, only three weeks after I left, the Isle was visited by an epidemic of 'flu to which the good priest, only 43 years of age, succumbed. When I had heard of his illness through John Duncan I had sent off at once some liquid restorative food, knowing that nothing of the sort could be got in the Isle. But he died before it arrived.

I had no time now to work on my tunes. I had no words either until later Dr. Alexander Carmichael, of *Carmina Gadelica* fame, himself visited Eriskay and secured for me some verses. And so the matter dropped for a time.

I could not revisit the Isles in the summer of 1906, but in my 1906-7 syllabus of lecture-recitals I included the 'Visit to the Outer Hebrides and Celtic Music'. And for this I had to prepare a number of the songs with English translation and pianoforte accompaniment.[1]

When, in 1882, in connexion with my father's Scots song tours, I had first taken up Gaelic song, I had used it only in the form of three-part unaccompanied vocal trios for female voices. It was not until 1895, for the Summer Meeting Celtic recitals, that I tried it with pianoforte accompaniment, somewhat on the model of the Art Song.

In the interval I had been so occupied with the rendering and lecture-analysis of the finest Art Songs, in the course of which I had always separated the vocal melody from the accompanying figures, that I could no longer think a melody without at the same time thinking some possibly appropriate framework of musical design and colour. The possibilities of the latter are inexhaustible.[2]

These many years devoted to showing what the great song-writers could do in their settings of a simple vocal line of melody were surely my own best apprenticeship for the task of trying to blend traditional melody with appropriate harmonic setting.

The Ducoudray Breton volume, with all its strangely beautiful airs on unfamiliar scales, its poetically and musically suggestive pianoforte accompaniments, and its French singing transla-tions, had long before opened to my mind a vista of the possi-bilities there were of a new development in the direction of a *national Scoto-Celtic* song—an art song that should incorporate faithfully within itself our Scoto-Celtic melodic heritage, while at the same time growing organically out of the miniature forms which it thus enlarged and enframed.[3]

[1]The programme in 1907 included 'The Skye Fisher', 'The Mull Fisher', 'The Eriskay Lullaby', 'Hebridean Mother's Song'.

[2]Think but of Peter Cornelius's 'Ein Ton', in which the singer has but *one* note to sing throughout; and yet, with its pianoforte commentary, what a perfect song! And so the simplest Hebridean melody, like that of the milking song 'The Handsome Lad Frae Skye', may be drawn on by its harmonies and held together by a recurring rhythmical formula so as to deceive even an expert at first hearing (as I know) into believing it to be quite a long tune.

[3]I had quite early in my career dabbled in arrangements of Scots tunes. The published accompaniments to many of the Scots songs were often far from satisfactory. When they were *musicianly* (written by one who did not understand *songs)* they were often

Further, English singing words had to be provided. I had not yet got in touch with Kenneth Macleod, who later collaborated with me; so, *faute de mieux,* I myself wrote 'The Skye Fisher', 'The Mull Fisher', and others.

My first Hebridean recital, in February 1907, made such an impression that I not only straightway published one or two of the songs, with my piano settings and translations, but decided to resume the work of collecting seriously, as soon as possible.

My son David was at Edinburgh University. My daughter Patuffa was carrying on musical studies at the Matthay School in London. As I wanted her company to the Isle, I had to wait till near the end of her session, as well as my own, and it was not until the end of July that we were able to sail from Oban in the *Plover* for Lochboisdale. This time, on arrival we hired a trap from Mackenzie of the hotel there and drove the ten miles to Pollachar, the southerly point of Uist, a ten-mile drive through bog-land, the road very rough, not such as one would care to cycle over, and the island very low-lying.

This Isle of Uist, with all the other separate isles of what was once *the* Long Island, would seem to be slowly sinking, and there are tales of submerged church and graveyard still to be seen, on the west coast, at low tide.

At Pollachar we had to wait a while, watching from the windows of the upper parlour of the little inn before we saw the boat coming towards us from Eriskay, manned by my old friends Duncan of the *Sgeulachdan* and Dugald of the post office. We and our bags were soon on board, and a pleasant sail

---

overloaded. 'The artist is known at times by what he leaves out.' I have sometimes thought that an anthology of the most successful accompaniments to Scots songs would be a great boon to singers. In travelling concert days, besides vocal unaccompanied trios, I had made suites of Scots airs, mostly for four hands on the piano, and these, simple as they were, played with orchestral precision and *élan* brought down the house.

As programme manager, when we had a long run in one of the big cities, I was sometimes at my wits' end to provide sufficient variety from the existing store of traditional Scots melody. Had I had all the Hebridean songs since unearthed, what a wealth of choice they would have afforded! I remember hot nights in Sydney, after the evening concerts, sitting up late, late, trying to juggle a few fresh programmes out of the available material.

across found our old quarters awaiting us. Patuffa and myself were now the only visitors. The house at Rudha Ban was at that time the only private stone-and-lime-built structure in the Isle. We had wisely brought a good box of provisions with us. Eggs were plentiful, and we got milk, with fish occasionally. The potatoes not yet being ready, these we secured occasionally by the post. But we managed to exist fairly well, and Patuffa was in the highest spirits, bathing every day with only seals for 'Companions of the Bath', and riding the bare-backed ponies up perpendicular rocks, her feet in the empty creels that hung from their flanks. When not bathing, we pursued diligently, unintermittently, song-collecting-and-noting at any and every hour of the day.

The airs were gathered, for the most part, among the most natural, genuine, and uncorrupted people I have ever met, these dwellers in that lonely island of the Outer Hebrides.

'An ancient race, living until our days, and almost under our eyes, its own life in some obscure islands and peninsulas of the west, more and more affected by external influences, but still faithful to its own tongue, its own memories, its own customs, and its own genius'—this of Renan's, on the Celtic race as a whole, was singularly applicable to our own Scots Outer Hebridean islanders, and to the dwellers on our western peninsulas. And such memories, customs, tongue, genius, are crystallized in their songs. 'Nothing', says Renan, 'can equal the delicious sadness of the Celtic melodies; like emanations from above, they fall, drop by drop, upon the soul, and pass through it like the memories of another world.'

Over a century ago Wordsworth, listening to the solitary reaper 'breaking the silence of the seas among the farthest Hebrides', asked, 'Will no one tell me what she sings?' and wondered if the burden of her song may be 'of old, unhappy, far-off things', or of 'some natural sorrow, loss, or pain, that has been, and may be again'. But then, as now,

Whate'er the theme, the Maiden sang
As if her song could have no ending;

I saw her singing at her work,
And o'er the sickle bending.

And in a verse which has a place in more than one old Hebridean ballad, a solitary reaper, a deserted maiden, sings:

Feasgar foghair 's mi air achadh bhuana
Saoil sibh fein nach mi fhein bha truagh dheth,
A h-uile te 's a fear fhein ri 'guallainn,
'S mo leannan donn-sa, gur fada bhuam-s'e.

(An autumn evening and I on the fields of reaping
Think you not, was I not the sad one?
Every woman with her lad at her shoulder,
And my own brown-haired love afar from me.)

And there is another verse which I have heard coupled with this in an old song sung in the Outer Isles, a verse anent which W. B. Yeats has remarked: 'If men did not remember, or half remember, impossible things; and it may be, if the worship of the sun and the moon had not left a faint reverence behind it, should we find a Celtic maiden singing:

Thug thu sear dhiom is thug thu siar dhiom,
Thug thu ghealach is thug thu ghrian dhiom,
Thug thu'n cridhe a bha 'nam chliabh dhiom,
Cha mhor a ghaoil-ghil nach tug thu Dia dhiom.

(You have taken the East from me, you have taken the West from me,
You have taken the Moon from me,
You have taken the Sun from me,
And my fear is great, you have taken God from me)

Wordsworth, drinking in the beauty and the emotional burden of the reaper's lyric without following its literal sense, 'listened motionless and still', until, filled with the sudden strangeness and beauty of the Hebridean song, he slowly mounted the hill, while, as he tells us, 'the music in my heart I bore, long after it was heard no more'.

Such singing at work has unhappily passed away. But one day in Eriskay I did surprise a woman as she sang at her reaping (there are no fields there, only little patches of cultivated sand), and she was reaping, not with the sickle—the grain was too short—she was lifting it by handfuls, roots and all.

Milking-croons and waulking songs too can occasionally be heard, especially the latter, although with the disappearance of home spinning and handweaving the great musical ceremony of the waulking or shrinking of the woollen web is also forgotten and neglected. Many of the best of the songs are labour songs, such as rowing songs, churning songs, spinning songs, and waulking (or fulling) songs. Some of these, the latter particularly, are most exciting. I have seen the islanders while singing them seem to get hypnotized with their own rhythm, working themselves into a frenzy with it, and no one who has not witnessed it can realize what an intoxicating power strong rhythm can exercise over the Celtic temperament. By this 'tyranny of rhythm', says the Dean of Lismore, 'the folksongs of a race help to preserve its language'.

But the rhythms are not always those with which we are most familiar. Like the Finnish folk, who are partial to a five-beat rhythm, the Hebrideans indulge in strange combinations such as may be found in a milking song, which is in seven-beat time, and in a waulking song, which balances fives with threes. The seven-beat milking song (the words of which, by the way, had already been collected some forty years earlier by Alexander Carmichael and included in his *Carmina Gadelica*) was sung to me by one Peggy Macdonald, a dame who came across from South Uist to Eriskay on a visit to her friends on the island. She meant to stay a night or two, but was storm-stayed with us for over a week, greatly to my advantage, since living in the same house with her I was able to carry on the work of song-noting at all hours, beginning often in the morning before breakfast and filling in moments at odd times till the night was far spent. We were like-minded in our enthusiasm for Hebridean songs, and she listened with the keenest of interest to the graphophone records of songs I had collected from others, swiftly memorizing both words and music of such as took her fancy. She was a clever body, and justly proud of the fact that every one of her snod woollen garments was of her own carding, dyeing, spinning, and weaving!

As a help in the song-collecting this time we had brought with us a very small and easily portable recording graphophone with a good supply of wax cylindrical blank records. So now when we went down to the *ceilidhs* in the evening we could entertain the folk with the reproduction of their own voices while at the same time amassing valuable material for our work. (I must say here, however, that such records are not very reliable unless one has *heard* the song. Often the rhythm is lost, and at times the singer begins singing before the voice is directed towards the bell.) Patuffa proved an invaluable companion and helpmate with the graphophone. She appealed to the Gaels in appearance and manner: 'She is one of ourselves,' they said of her. She kept a diary in the form of letters to her Aunty Jessie, written every couple of days. Of a day spent across the Sound in Uist, where we were collecting from Penny O'Henley, she writes: 'As mother had forgotten her glasses, I tried my hand at taking down, and my word it was difficult, as the time and scale are both so different from modern music.' And again, 'Mother has just had me in the kitchen to help take down such a queer song, and as we have now succeeded I can go on with my letter.' And later, 'I have again had to help mother with a queerer song, but I'll get my letter finished this time'.

The younger women of the Isles are at all times in great request at east coast fishings. Famous for speed and skill in barrelling herring, they are secured long ahead of time for the mainland herring-fishings. Hence we found few of them at home, and our singers were mainly young men and old women.

In the home of Gillespie of the Skye Fisher tune we had many a *ceilidh,* his father smiling benignly on us, greatly pleased that his son had been singled out for his songs. To use our graphophone here we had to place it as evenly as possible on top of a great kist, a wee three-legged stool placed in front of the kist serving to seat the singer. One night, after our hostess, the *cailleach,*[1] had quitted the stool and the reproducing needle had

[1] Old dame, pronounced *calyach.*

been put on, an intelligent inquisitive chicken hopped down from the rafters, took its place on the stool, and listened enraptured with its ear at the bell to the voice of its mistress. No doubt it had 'assisted' at many a *ceilidh*.

The forenoons as a rule were not good for song collecting, so we spent the time sea-bathing or climbing the hill, Patuffa on the creel pony. 'To-day,' she writes, 'we went up the hill for peats. For the third time I rode on the pony's back, with my feet in the creels and hanging on to her mane. As she was very frisky, she chose the steepest parts and went straight up instead of from side to side. I cannot describe what it was like, going up the hill, over rocks and through bogs, on this small pony's back. Mother could not look at me, she was so frightened. Through it all I stuck on and did not get off until we arrived at the peats. And then what a view! We saw Skye, Rhum, Canna, Eigg, and even the mainland! It was a perfect day.'

In another letter she writes: 'Edinburgh isn't in it with wind. When the wind blows here—which it does most of the time—it would fain take everything along with it. We are sitting in a sheltered spot, on the rocks down in a sandy bathing bay, and the sun is pouring down upon us, but before we can get back to the house we will have to go through a gale. We never wear hats, but when necessary little shawls over our heads, as every one else does here.'

One night, in a gale of wind, we crossed the few yards separating our house from the presbytery, where the Rev. John Macneill was in residence as successor to Father Allan. His sister Annie Macneill was a fine singer, and she gave us a number of songs on the graphophone—their mother was a native of the lone Isle of Saundray and from her they had got many old songs. On our way back, Patuffa records that 'we came across again at 10 o'clock, hardly able to stand against a gale of wind and rain, which continued all through the night'. The use of the graphophone was gay enough when all went well, but the notation of the song was another matter. 'On Saturday morning', she writes, 'we made our first attempt at taking down a song from the graphophone, and, do you know, we got wildly excited. In the end we got it down, but not till we had struggled with it a long time.' 'Yesterday, early in the afternoon, we went down to the post office with the graphophone again to get more songs. Three of the fishermen were there and they went on singing songs till eleven o'clock. We filled seven records, each with three or four tunes, and by the time we were finished, both of us were quite exhausted, having had nothing to eat since very early in the afternoon. On the strength of it all, mother had her breakfast in bed this morning!' Yes, it was fatiguing work. 'Over and over again we wished we had absolute pitch. If we can't hit upon the right note to begin with we are lost. We often say to each other we shall have to go home soon for a holiday, because as long as we are here we won't be able to stop taking down songs.'

Patuffa was unwearying. Patience, patience, patience, is essential in delicate work of this kind, working as we often had to do on the long undisturbed depths of an aged mind. Patuffa sat so quietly with me in the little cottages and was so indefatigable in her manipulation of the graphophone that I hardly knew she was there. Things seemed to happen if I but wished them. Two, or at times three, little tunes could be recorded on one cylinder, if we did not sacrifice space to repetitions of verse and chorus. But never one cylinder was allowed by the little singing and listening company to be replaced in its padded case until it had been submitted to the reproducing needle and listened to by all, sometimes with great glee. This necessitated constant readjustment, alternately, of the two needles; (or disks); a matter of great anxiety, for in the moisture-laden atmosphere of the Isles the graphophone was apt to go out of order. In the very middle of an exciting and productive *séance* it would refuse to budge. A small unreliable affair (a heavier instrument could not have been carried over bog and tussock), it caricatured the voices and rendered all the songs with an old man's wheeze, whence its nickname among the young lads was the *Bodach*.[1]

---

[1] Old cronie, pronounced *bóttach*.

Needless to say there are many variants of airs, of the favourite ancient airs, and one has to use one's judgement in selecting or collating from these a final version for publication. Father Allan did not approve of the graceless versions of many tunes as they appear in print. The old traditional singer, if an artist at all, was ever at liberty (indeed was expected) to use ornament to any extent and to improvise on the ancient theme much as the Hindus' authenticated singer is expected to do with the ancient Hindu 'Rags'.

That the folk are not only free, alike in the treatment of the melodic outline, the form, and the ornament of their songs, but that they are rhythmically strong enough to use freedom with the metrical accents, is evidenced by their happy use of syncopation.[1]

I shall not soon forget my delight on first hearing the 'Mermaid's Croon'.[2] The Rev. John Macneill, to whom I owe many a courtesy and the words of many a song, kindly took my daughter and myself over one afternoon to the Uist shore, whither many of my old Eriskay friends had migrated. The Isle of Eriskay being overcrowded, many of the crofters and fishermen were glad of the chance which offered to take up new crofts on South Uist.

Among these new settlers was one of the best singers of the island, Mrs. O'Henley, née Penny Macdonald. I was very anxious to meet her again, as she had many fine songs. Her husband's croft lay some distance back from the shore, and to reach it we had a tramp through a cold bog and a scramble up a brae face. As the croft was but newly taken up, the cottage was not yet built. We saw a great cairn of dry peats burning above a

[1] As in a slow rowing song in our first volume. Miss Frances Tolmie, from whom I noted this slow rowing song in the spring of 1908, says: 'The good old woman Oighrig Pheatan (or Effie Beaton) who sang it to me in 1861 was then about 80 years of age. Her period of youth would fall in the eighteenth century, when men still sang at their work. She remembered her mother telling her about the visit of Dr. Johnson to Ullinish, in the parish of Bracadale, in Skye, where she was in service. She was fond of commenting on the famous author's love of tea, and remembered how one morning this remarkable English gentleman drank eighteen cups to breakfast.'

[2] In volume 1, not the Eriskay Lullaby, but the other: 'Sleep Beneath the Foam o' the Waves'.

114

huge grey boulder, and were told that by to-morrow the rock would be split by the heat of the smouldering turf, and be ready for use in the building of the walls. Meantime, for the summer months, the mother and bairns were being housed in a freshly put together turf sheiling, a most primitive shelter, but wherever this beautiful woman sat with a baby on her knee, there you had a living picture of the Madonna and Child. She was sitting by the peat fire, surrounded by her bairns, when we entered; and we sat on the little three-legged stool by her fire as she crooned songs to her baby and to us. This 'Mermaid's Croon' was the last she sang, and I listened with delight and astonishment as she gave the little syncopated lullaby with the perfect feeling for rhythm which comes apparently from a lifelong association of music with labour. Before I could get it noted, however, our crew reappeared, hurried us off, carried us aboard, hoisted sail, and were out into the Sound before we could draw breath. The Eriskay tide waits for no man.

However, she herself came over to Eriskay to attend service at the chapel, and I got the little tune noted from her as she sat on a rock waiting for a boat to carry her across again to the Uist Shore.

22

Barra. Collecting on the East Coast (1907-8)

Patuffa and I were to leave Eriskay by Barra, sailing south-wards. 'As far as songs go', wrote Patuffa, 'we have plenty, it merely depends on the weather how long we stay in Barra.' How little we reckoned on what lay before us! From Barra have come many, very many of our finest songs.

One Sunday morning, just before we left Eriskay, I was in old John McInnes's house. He gathered his household under his wing and 'gaed aff' to the kirk like any good old Scots Presbyterian, and I was left by the fire with the good wife. She sang to me (shall I ever forget it?) the Christ Child's Lullaby. Surely, if I had recovered only this one beautiful lull-song, my pilgrimage to the Isles had not been in vain.

That afternoon, service over and the seamen free, John Mac-neill bade them get ready a boat to take him with Patuffa and myself over to Barra. It was a sunshiny afternoon, and our track lay between small islands where the seals lay thick on the ledges basking in the sun—it was Sunday. They made no movement until our boat was close upon them, the great patriarch seal haughtily remaining on the rock until, at the last moment, he too remembered that discretion is the better part of valour and slid gracefully into the sea.

We landed from the open boat at North Bay in Barra, whence Patuffa and I walked to Allt on the east coast. We had been ad-vised to make our head-quarters there. Here, with the help of Mrs. Joseph Maclean, Skallary, we got some songs during a stay of two days, notably the 'Fairy Plaint', sung into our grapho-phone by a little old woman with a sweet thread of voice—it takes breathless listening at the graphophone bell to hear it—and when asked where she got the song she replied (looking as though she thought it a strange question), from the 'bean anns a bhrugh': the woman in the burrow (or fairy mound).[1] And that same fairy mound lies in the pass or *bealach* that leads from this rocky east coast of the isle to the sandy west. And there are to-day folks, native and otherwise, who tell me that they still hear fairy music there.[2] This little old woman's Fairy Plaint has a most haunting recurrent high note, typical of much of the oldest Barra melodic stuff. The natives of Barra have always been famed as sea-faring folk. Did they get from sea-faring men of the northern seas some Scandinavian ways of music-thinking, or did the Norse rather, in their traffic with the Isles, borrow themes and motifs from the Gaels? Wagner, anyhow,[3] seems to have borrowed some of his themes and motifs showing kinship with Hebridean melody from the sea-faring songs of the Norse sailors, with whom he came in contact in his young manhood on a stormy voyage of three weeks in the Northern seas.

We had been warned in Oban that Castle Bay, the chief port of Barra, was now too sophisticated to yield us ancient songs, hence our stay in the north of the isle. But on the afternoon of the last day of our stay, while Patuffa and I were resting in the sun on the rocks at Allt, I seemed suddenly to understand that we must without delay go on to Castle Bay and work there. Fortunately I acted immediately on the impulse and went straight to our host, the lobster-fisher at Allt, and found that he could drive us in at once.

Climbing a steep hill that lay between us and the port, we

---

[1] That the mound-dwellers had music of their own, and that the Gaelic-speaking dwellers above ground borrowed it when they got the chance, is implied in many an old folk-tale. *Sian,* soft sorrowful music issued from the green knoll, and the 'slender women of the green kirtles and the yellow hair' sang lullabies and love-songs.

[2] There is certainly some strange quality in the island environment. 'Intelligence', says Bergson, 'should take the risk of a plunge into the phosphorescent water around it.'

[3] The recurrent high note of Senta's ballad in *The Flying Dutchman* is evidently a reminiscence of the music heard on this sea-trip.

came suddenly on a magnificent view revealing the town and the bay lying far below us, dark purple isles looming seaward.

We got in touch at once with John Macneill's father, Michael Macneill, the chief merchant in the Bay, told him we were sailing to-morrow morning at noon: could he help us to hear the best singers and the best of the old songs? He was delighted, promised to gather the singers together in his store to-morrow morning, and with that we rested. Castle Bay, Barra, is a very hub of civilization compared with the little Isle of Eriskay; and a hot bath and a roast chicken for supper that night are memories the delight of which only those who have roughed it can share.[1]

Well, next morning in Castle Bay we had one of the most exciting *séances* of our song-collecting career. Michael Macneill might have been specially commissioned for the job, he was so efficient. He had sent round the fiery cross, so to speak, the singers were all gathered in his store on the quay (it is now the post office), and he himself acted as master of ceremonies.

He took from his pocket a note-book in which he had entered a list of the most noteworthy of the ancient traditional songs of Barra and its dependent islets, and he called on each singer in turn, making choice himself of what they should sing. They were all old women—women who had never left the Isles, spoke no English, and were still as true to the old traditions as they might have been two or three hundred years earlier. Our graphophone had been placed on the smooth even surface of the store counter where Patuffa officiated. A great crowd stood inside, others craned their necks from outside, all eager to listen and adjudicate at this festival. Ducoudray himself could not have fared better with his Government commission in Brittany than I did that morning under command of Michael Macneill.

The most valuable find that morning was undoubtedly 'Kishmul's Galley'. The singer was a woman from the smaller

[1]Among other such impressions that remain I recall the deliciousness of the plain bread and butter that Lizzie and I had served to us in our own room in the hotel at Kimberley the afternoon we arrived there, after riding for weeks over the veldt in Boerland, living on salt mutton, pumpkin, tinned butter, and sour dough.

rock isle of Mingulay. I had intended visiting this island, which lies south of Barra—John Macneill was to have taken us in an open boat—but the weather was too stormy that summer, and we were told that if we attempted it we would have to be thrown ashore like mail-bags! The isle is indeed no more than a bare rock in the swirl of the Atlantic. So greedy is this swirl that it robs the rock even of its seaweed. But the islemen, nothing daunted, were wont to fetch the needful wrack-manure from other shores, and in rare quiet weather carry it on their shoulders, walking breast deep in the water, to the shore. Is it to be wondered at that eventually the islemen abandoned Mingulay and raided the accessible isle of Vatersay?

I was disappointed that we could not land at Mingulay. But had we done so, we might have missed the best singer of that isle, as she was presently beside us on the mainland of Barra —Barra is twelve miles in circumference—and she it was that morning who was called on by Michael Macneill to sing to us 'Latha dhomh am Beinn a Cheathaich', the song I have called 'Kishmul's Galley'.

In order to get records of as many airs as possible, we generally made a practice of taking only one verse and chorus on the cylinder, but fortunately in this case (and in that of 'Hebrid Seas') we took a number of verses, and in doing so got some valuable variants. In my published version of 'Kishmul' I give three forms of the melody, all noted accurately from that record, and forming in themselves a most valuable example of the consummately artistic treatment by the singer of a given theme. Another song we heard here was 'The Ballad of Macneill of Barra', attributed to a Mingulay woman who lived some centuries ago. She was named Nic Iain Aoidh (the daughter of John of the Isles). I was told by a Mingulay fisher that the tradition runs that she had her 'gift' from the Master of the Black Art. The Evil One[1] asked when bestowing it, it is said, whether she would sing to please herself or to please others. Fiercely

[1] Another tradition has it that she got the 'gift' from a *leannan sith,* a fairy lover.

119

independent, she chose to please herself. No one, said Hector Macphie, my informant, could endure her singing! But she was victorious in a song-contest between herself and a Uist woman, and this Barra Ballad was the song she sang in Uist itself. The tale has it that at the end of the singing, when the vanquished singer dropped senseless from chagrin, the incensed Uist people would have bound Nic Iain Aoidh. But she escaped from them, ran to the shore where her boat lay moored, drew a knife from her bosom, cut the boat adrift, and was off to Barra before they could lay hands on her again. Song-contests in those days did not make for an *entente cordiale* between rival islands.

I shall never forget hearing such songs from the old Mingulay woman with a voice, face, and bearing expressive alike of independence, gaiety, and strength, nor the latent capacity for fierce joy to be seen in the eyes of these people who lived in a world of wind and wave turmoil on lonely ocean rocks, where the air sweeps with intoxicating swiftness and energy, and the sea beats with a fascinating defiance.

The Castle Bay song function over, we had to get on board a small steamer for Dunvegan, where we were due, *en route* for Uig, Skye.

At Uig we were guests of one of Patuffa's friends, whose husband had rented Conan Lodge for the shooting. But here I found that song-research was barely possible in such conditions. Our hostess was keen enough, but our successful host thought me quite mad when I sneaked off at the civilized dinner-hour of eight to trudge some miles in the rain to a fisher's hut (I could find him at home only at this hour), where I heard and noted Clanranald's Parting Song.

Returned to the mainland, I paid a visit to my friend Jane Hay, at St. Abb's Haven on the east coast. Here I met Rutland Boughton, the composer, since so well known because of the great popular success of his *Immortal Hour*. I showed him and sang to him some of the Hebridean songs we had collected and set, and he was ravingly enthusiastic over them. He was the first creative musician to be touched by their beauty. To Percy

Scholes, the English music-missionary as we might perhaps call him, he wrote on the back of an envelope which Scholes forwarded to me: 'I myself place these with the few greatest things in music—the "48", the *Choral Symphony,* and *Parsifal.* The accompaniments are the perfection of folksong atmosphere. The composer is a real genius.' Surely never any one got such encouragement to go on.

Boughton tells me that he then proposed to work up some of the material into an opera or music drama, but I was not then enthusiastic about the scheme. That he therefore turned to Fiona Macleod's work for inspiration along Hebridean lines, the outcome in the end being his *Immortal Hour.* However, when he returned to Birmingham he inoculated Granville Bantock with the virus of his enthusiasm, and Bantock has been faithful to his love of it through many vicissitudes.

In the house party at St. Abb's that summer there were a number of other English visitors. A picnic party was got up one afternoon to drive to Eyemouth, a fishing village near, in order that they might see the herring-curing.

In conversation I learned from one of the curers that they had some crews of island girls among their workers. I asked him to take me to them—work was finished for the day. But first he had to take me to see his own wife, as she would be proud to receive one of the Kennedys.

When I asked if the Highland girls had any songs, he answered 'No'; then as an afterthought added, 'Oh yes, they have some nonsense of their own.' After quite an hour, I got him to lead me at last to the lodging of the island girls. They goodnaturedly sang me one or two good and to me unfamiliar airs, including 'Hebrid Seas' (or 'Heman dubh'). I wanted that tune. What was my chagrin to find that I had neither pencil nor paper! I might have bought these in the village? I had not a penny in my pocket; I was out with an afternoon picnic party; where was my party? They had driven back to St. Abb's apparently hours ago. I was hungry, too; couldn't buy a biscuit. There was nothing for it but to thank the girls, tell them I hoped

121

to see them again, and hungrily face the walk home in the gathering darkness, miles over the cliffs. And the girls were leaving for the Outer Isles (the Lewes) the day after to-morrow. I was not to be beaten. Next morning I wired my son in Edinburgh to join me at Eyemouth with the graphophone. On the very day they were to leave for the Isles, I called again on the girls. They were all in a state of the greatest excitement, packing their kists for the homeward voyage. No, they had no time now to sing songs. I suggested that they might listen perhaps while they packed. So David set up the graphophone on the table in the centre of the room and we let them hear one of their own island songs, sung by one of their own folk. In a moment all was changed. They forgot their packing, they crowded round the graphophone, they laughed till the tears came, they were each ready and eager to sing, and it needed no pressure now to get a record of 'Heman dubh'. I have given this in volume 1 as 'Hebrid Seas', and fortunately we took several verses of it, the variant verse III in the published version being exactly as recorded that day on the cylinder. The repetition in that last verse of one of the motifs is typical and is another instance of the free renderings customary among musical singers in the Isles. This traditional Celtic art, as I said before, would seem to be much the same in this respect as that of the ancient Hindus.

We got other songs from them, but this 'Hebrid Seas' was the outstanding find that day.

A curious result of our long stay in the Isles and our obsession with the ancient music there was that when Patuffa returned to London and to her pianoforte studies at the Matthay School she felt her sense of tonality temporarily out of step, so to speak, especially with Beethoven.

Now from her infancy, when as a little crawler she lived under my Bechstein while I made music on it, she had always recognized and preferred Beethoven. Oh her return from the Isles she found that it took some time to readjust herself to Beethoven, whereas she had no difficulty whatever with Chopin.

Some of the songs I had got on my first visit to the Isles I had already published separately, and the work was beginning to be known. A Pan-Celtic Congress, held that same autumn in Edinburgh, invited Margaret and myself to give a lecture-recital in illustration of my work. We gave it in the Synod Hall, and there we had in our audience Alfred Perceval Graves, Ernest Rhys, and Mrs. William Sharp, all well known in literary and Celtic circles. This was my first meeting with the widow of 'Fiona Macleod'. She took at once the love of her heart for me, showed an intense interest in my work, and encouraged me enthusiastically to continue it. A radiant personality, she seemed ever to shed strength and courage around her.

Alfred Perceval Graves mentioned my work to Arthur Boosey, the head of the song-publishing firm. I was invited to give examples of our work at a Pan-Celtic gathering in London early in 1908. Arthur Boosey, having sent his representative to report, asked me to call, and thereupon undertook the publication of volume 1, which was already partly engraved.[1]

In the spring of 1908 I had to cross the Minch earlier than usual in order to go on the hunt for the words of the airs I had collected there the previous summer. Unwittingly, this spring, I had gone at the very busiest season of the year, when the herring-fishing and the digging over of the croft-land occupied old and young, men and women alike, and when song-collecting was out of the question till darkness drove the weary field-workers home for the night. Unthinking people, Mrs. Maclean at Skallary remarked to me, will tell you that the islanders are lazy; and yet, she said, look round you at this time of the year and you will see that the whole island is dug over like a garden. And as I walked back by Brevaig to Castle Bay I saw men and women toiling with the spade in the black earth, lonely figures, bulking largely in the picture (the fields were so small); and every here and there a blaze of colour, where a sudden black

[1] I had worked for two years and more without any Gaelic collaborator. Hence the first volume contains things that Kenneth Macleod is not responsible for, and also some rough literal translations which he sent not for publication but for my guidance. These I unwittingly engraved.

patch was being spread with the gorgeous red-brown and ivory-white seaweed which is used for manure. The sea and land in Barra are inseparable playmates, and the sea-wrack for the fields is found close at hand and fetched easily on the back of the creel-girt ponies.[1]

The preservation of the old traditional song-lore has its roots probably in the peculiar physical and social environment of the people. In those remote isles, perhaps just because one still finds life on the material side as simple as at the earlier stages of social organization, one finds a people hindered, it is true, by physical conditions from producing a material civilization, yet the more free of their emotions and imagination. Incredibly hard are the physical conditions on some of the smaller Isles. Into the rocky hollows a little sandy soil is wind-drifted, the self-same crops grown year after year, the drifting sand probably bringing with it the needful supply of vital elements. The age-long communism which has left us this heritage of song was held together by ties of blood-relationship and was free from wage labour. Even to-day, in the small Isles, if you cannot cut your own peats you cannot easily secure hired labour to do it. Yet if that ancient civilization is fast dying out, its tale of folk-art still yields 'the flower of its ideals'.[2]

A late spring that year for the potato-planting clashing with the opening of the fishing season, all hands were called for, and never until after the daylight failed could I get any one to sit down and sing to me. After a week of fruitless effort I was finally rewarded on the last possible day of my stay. I was recommended to Annie Johnson,[3] schoolmistress there and herself a native of Barra. From that day to this she has been my valued friend and my invaluable collaborator. It was a Tuesday, and I was to leave the Island through the night some time. The little steamer comes in and departs again sometime among the 'sma'

---

[1]This cannot be said to hold true of all the Isles. Far otherwise, indeed, was it with the neighbouring Isle of Mingulay, a bare rock in the swirl of the Atlantic.
[2]W. B. Yeats.
[3]The Johnsons are MacIains who have anglicized their name.

124

oors'. Annie Johnson, when I met her and begged her help, said: 'Come to our cottage at eight and bring the phonograph with you.' Which I did. She lived a good mile out of the town. I found her mother and two bright old dames, experts all in the old songs, awaiting me. Annie, with pencil and note-book, wrote in Gaelic to the dictation of one of the isleswomen, and got from her, among other things, the Gaelic words of 'Kishmul's Galley', while I made graphophone records from the other tunes and refrains.

We worked in the lamp-lit kitchen until 11 o'clock, when, gathering up the spoils and thanking the clever old dames and wishing them *oidhche mhath,* we started down the hill again. The night was black dark, the rain was falling heavily, the road was thick with *glaur.* We had to do the mile and more to the pier guided by the glare of a burning peat, held high upon a pointed stick by Annie Johnson herself. I was tired. I had been advised by my hostess, Mrs. McKinnon, a successful merchant, to go to bed, as her shop-lad, she said, would remain awake and warn me of the steamer's approach. Alas, I slept only too well, and awoke at three in the morning to hear voices of folk passing beneath my window. In my attempt to reach it, I knocked over the candle and matches. In answer to my cry, 'Is the steamer in?' came the reply, 'Been in some time, leaving shortly'. What a hurried scramble it was in the dark, getting dressed and getting my things together! With hastily drawn-on shoes and overshoes I shuffled along to the pier-head with some of my bags. 'Would they wait until I went back for the remainder?' 'Yes, if I would hurry up.' So I shuffled back, and shouldering my case of graphophone records slithered along the wet quay and reached the little steamer just before she steamed off. But I was happy. I had my words. 'Kishmul's Galley' was safe now for all time.

23

Collaboration with
Kenneth Macleod (Begun 1908)

Until the late spring of 1908 I had never met Kenneth Macleod and only shortly before had been put in touch with him. I had long felt the need of a reliable Gaelic editor, and appealed to Professor McKinnon at Edinburgh University for help. He said, 'There is only *one* man, Kenneth Macleod.' 'Yes,' I replied, 'but I have heard he is too busy to work with me.' 'Write him to-night,' said the professor, 'and if you do not hear from him to-morrow, saying he will be delighted to collaborate, I shall be surprised.' And so it was. Kenneth Macleod, from that day, not only edited the material I collected but added liberally from his own stores. To him now went the words of the songs noted at the Castle Bay *ceilidh* from the dear old singers who soon after were 'gathered to their fathers'.

When I returned, he (stationed at Straloch at the time) joined me in Edinburgh and we worked over the material, preparing it for publication. Preparation of singing translations and adaptations we mainly do together, he giving the basic fabric in English and I putting it through the test of singing. I suggest modifications perhaps, although in some cases the lines are entirely his, in others entirely my own.[1] It is a thrilling experience working with him on the material I bring home yearly from my song-forays in the Isles. I gather and write with great care the valuable syllabic refrains polished by generations of communal use,

[1] Words for singing are not intended to be read. The test of song-words lies in the singing.

126

and with these I note also such verse-lines as may still cling fragmentarily to the tunes. In this matter we are very thrifty, Kenneth and I. We preserve all the good lines, single words even, from the Gaelic originals, and piece these together—as Burns did 150 years ago in Lowland song, and with Burns's aim, that of preserving the old airs and keeping them in currency. 'Better mediocre words to a tune than none at all' wrote Burns. The old puirt a bial (mouth tunes) have frequently none at all. For instance, the words to the tune I used for 'To People Who Have Gardens' were but a string of Christian names. These in *the Gaelic* had rhythmic and resonant value. But what of their English equivalents? In the case of ancient, classical, heroic lore a literal translation is called for, but to translate literally, or even to paraphrase, songs which owe their popularity and longevity merely to a felicitous musicalness of language in the original is beside the mark. The technique of song-writing, indeed, is quite different in its nature from literal translation or from the writing of lyrics intended to be spoken or perhaps only to be read by the eye. Song words must sing well; else you may lay them, and their tunes, on the shelf.

In the many cases where there is something of value in the original, Kenneth lets it filter through his own mind and gets the essence of it sometimes—the Gaels themselves have admitted this—in a more beautiful form than in the original.

There are cases where fine words and tunes have, in course of time, drifted apart. 'Caristiona' was a song the words of which Kenneth valued so much that he begged me to set it. The melody he crooned to it, however, was so poor that I refused over and over again to attempt this. At the same time, I had in my portfolio a tune for which I desperately wanted words. I had only one line of verse. We separately carried these about in our portfolios for years, until one day we discovered that my one line of verse belonged to his fine verses. So at last we brought melody and words together again, and 'Caristiona' proved one of the finest songs of our collection.

It is a mistake to suppose that the Gaelic words in every case pre-dated the English. The English version of 'Benbecula Bridal' was written by me some time before Kenneth wrote his 'An Triall Bainnse', a Gaelic idealized version of the same theme. I had written the words on the very spot where I had heard the tune, the verses directly inspired by the bridal procession which started out across the Machair from the very croft of the *cailleach* from whose singing I had noted it. Kenneth wrote his Gaelic words some time afterwards.[1] Our song-word collaboration is frequently a real joint effort. In other words, we touch up each other's essays. He supplied me with *one* syllable in the Benbecula song—*sea* in *sea*-laughter, and I put the finishing touch to his 'Dance to Your Shadow' by adding the *second* half to each verse.

A large proportion of the songs have literal or almost literal singing translations. Of these 'Kishmul's Galley', my own translation, is literal, save that I have omitted merely the local sixteenth-century names of the men on board the vessel; 'The Seagull of the Land-under-Waves' is a condensed version of the original; 'The Death Croon' gives the English in full; as do also 'Sea Sorrow', 'The Harper', 'Sea Longing', 'Heartling of my Heart', 'The Birlinn of the White Shoulders', 'The Fairy Plaint', 'The Hebridean Sea-Reivers', 'Sea Sounds', 'The Lord of the Isles', and 'The Harris Love Lament'.

Sometimes we manage to make a singable and at the same time very close translation. I myself have done this, I think, in one or two of the lighter labour lilts such as 'The Weaving Lilt' and 'The Potato-lifting', the Gaelic of which I got from Annie Johnson in Barra. When I first sang my translations of these to her, she nearly doubled up with laughter, so tickled was she by the closeness of my version to the original. 'The Crone's Lilt' is another almost literal rendering, one which I did for my own singing, as also 'The Islay Reaper' for Patuffa. 'The Crone's Creel', on the other hand, is an original song which I made for the sake of the beautiful air. My other original song-words to

[1] A like case is 'The Skye Fisher'. My words were written first. In this case Kenneth Macleod's words, 'Tir nan Og', bear no relation to mine.

128

tunes that were in need include: 'Land of Heart's Desire', 'The Mull Fisher', 'Skye Fisher', 'Island Sheiling Song', and 'In Hebrid Seas'. The last is descriptive of my own sailing from Eriskay by Barra and Lochboisdale (in south Uist) to Dunvegan in Skye. My English words to the 'Sheiling Song' and 'The Mull Fisher' were both inspired by the first line of the original Gaelic verses, but follow these no further.

In many cases where the song-words are new they are not so new after all, since they have been, as Kenneth Macleod himself puts it, distilled from the old lore.

Some such process must inevitably take place in any renascence of traditional national song, especially when, like ours, it has been spilt almost as badly as the Humpty Dumpty of nursery rhyme, and now all the King's horses and all the King's men cannot put it together again.

Singing adaptations I have made occasionally from already existing fine translations of old lore, such as Thomas Pattison's 'Ossian's Midsummer Dream', from which I distilled 'Sleeps the Noon in the Deep Blue Sky'; and Sheriff Nicolson's version of that greatest of sea-poems, 'The Birlinn of Clanranald', by Alexander Macdonald.

Here and there in the Outer Isles I have come across lines of the chants (still persisting with their tunes) the words of which were written down in his research notebooks, fifty years ago, by Dr. Alexander Carmichael. From these, gathered into his famous *Carminia Gadelica,* I have been permitted by his daughter, Mrs. E. C. Watson, to eke out the otherwise scanty supply of words available to-day. Our seven-beat 'Milking Croon' and 'Churning Lilt' owe something to this.

Kenneth has taken a peculiar pleasure in seeking for fragments of poems traditionally attributed to Mary Macleod, the famous Island song-maker and singer of the sixteenth and seventeenth centuries. Born and buried in the Outer Isles, probably in Rodel in Harris, she wandered all over the Isles in the course of her 105 years and has left behind her a name for songs and song-lore. Did she make any of the tunes? Who knows? Ernest Newman once said to me that if he had the time, he believed he could single out from our wealth of Hebridean melodies those that must have been the creation of one great genius, one great *man;* and I for sheer contrariness replied, 'Why not one great *woman?*' But I do not think Mary Macleod was that one great musical genius. I think we must look farther back, and that the great framework-tunes, those that with their great syllabic refrains are ready for ever fresh verse lines (as the bard may arise), may have come down from centuries before even Mary Macleod's day.

When I was in South Harris in August 1927, song-hunting with Kenneth Macleod (it was the first time we had been together in the Outer Isles), he asked every one we met what they knew of Mary Macleod, and from their cordial answers one might have concluded that it was the day before yesterday, and not 300 years ago, that Mary had moved to and from the isle of her birth.

From a sea poem of hers, long ago entered into his notebook, we selected lines for our tunes 'Sea Feast', 'Sea Procession', 'To the Sea-King of the Isles', and 'Macleod's Galley'. The tunes were all crying out for words of that calibre, and who knows but that they may well have belonged to each other in the long ago, as did the words and tune of 'Caristiona'?

It is not easy to define our joint editorial and reconstructive work on the literary side, but the musical side is my own. Mention should, however, be made of the traditional airs I have noted from Kenneth Macleod's singing, airs which he had memorized consciously or unconsciously in his youth. These include the unique 'Spinning Song', 'The Death Croon', and 'Deirdre's Farewell'.

In making use of our melodic material I have, in a few instances, combined two or more melodies in one song, as in 'Sea Moods', 'Birlinn of Clanranald', 'Barra Love Lilt', 'Sea Quest', 'The Seal Maiden', 'Death Keening of a Hero'; and lastly 'Sea Tangle', in which I have incorporated four different melodies, each singly associated with the words.

130

For what I might have to say on the form and tonality of the Hebridean tunes, I must refer the reader to the introductions to my four volumes. In these I treat of scales and form. When I was in America in 1916, a critic in the *Boston Transcript* gave my first volume a most kindly review. But he found that with a woman's frailty I was given apparently to exaggeration, since I seemed to claim twelve different scales for the Island tonality. On that same day I received a letter from M. Duhamel, the French expert in Celtic (Breton) music, and he found that I, in his opinion, had understated the number, as he computed it at eighteen.

Duhamel, by the way, urged me to publish all the airs I got, for the sake of the musicologue. And this I have done in the introductions referred to, where I give all the tunes I had noted, although not yet set with words or harmonies.

Of Kenneth Macleod's 'Road to the Isles', by the way, which has become so popular as now to be a universal community song, I should explain that it was a *pièce d'occasion,* written in 1915 at my request as a tramping song for the Scots lads then somewhere in France. Kenneth and I were seated one evening on either side of the low fire in my music-room, with Calum Johnson (from Barra) playing on his chanter. He played us many airs from the Isles, and among them this version *of his own* of a tune he had learnt from an old tinker out there. I at once said to Kenneth, 'Do write something "swanky" to that for the lads in France.' So when he went home he wrote and sent it to me. The title and the idea of the song are entirely original. (There was no Gaelic model, although he himself has written a Gaelic version since for those who wished it.) In the song he carries the homesick lad, with poetic licence, by Tummel and Loch Rannoch to Morar. Why does he begin and end thus? Because Tummell and Loch Rannoch (the Gateway of the Western Highlands) are where my forefathers lived and died; and because Morar looks across to Eigg, where Kenneth Macleod himself was born.

At the time of working with Kenneth Macleod on our first

131

volume, I was a very busy professional woman. From my own hurried letters to Patuffa (at that time pursuing musical studies at the Matthay School in London), I find constant references to my state of overwork:

> 'I am writing to you to-day before breakfast. I have a pupil from Berwick at nine—a pupil comes to-day also from Carlisle.'
> 'Am hopelessly busy as usual. I think I shall have to retire and devote myself entirely to song-arranging and collecting . . . I can't find time even to note all the songs from the records we made in the Isles.'
> 'You must forgive me, my dearie, for not writing oftener—I have been worked to death and got bad headaches all the time and do not sleep well at nights, and so seeing friends and having cracks and writing friendly letters is to be denied onself. . .'
> 'I am very happy but very busy—although I may not write I am never forgetting you. Have just been drawing out pro-grammes for Lecture-Recital engagements here and there and have arranged one or two of our "Songs of the Hebrides".'

Besides my teaching, which began as a rule at 9 a.m., I was, as I have already stated, chief musical critic of the Edinburgh *Evening News*. This was no sinecure. My own original work had to be done through the night, between 10 p.m. and 2 a.m., and this burning the candle at both ends had to be paid for in the long run. But the necessary constant alertness of the musical sense was an asset; listening critically richly supplied my mind with material: appropriate though simple harmonic progres-sions, figured motifs, etc.,—in short, with the richly varied modern devices available for the setting of fine melodies.

I very much feared at one time that I should not be able to stand the strain. I wrote to Patuffa: 'Got home last night at 8 p.m., had dinner, went on to the "Orchestral"—came home, wrote critique—began teaching this morning at 9. . . . I spend much of my time at present wondering what I must give up. I can't make up my mind to give up the *Evening News*. . . Writing is a positive pain to me at present and I have hosts of it to do.'

I well remember one night walking along George Street, where we lived, and saying to myself, 'This cannot go on. What will

132

you give up?' And I decided to give up my work as musical critic. Curiously enough, this decision brought me such relief that I did not give it up, but carried on until the war relieved me of it automatically. Our first volume was now nearing completion. I wrote to Patuffa in June 1908: 'Songs of the Hebrides nearly finished now—am sending the 37th song to-day to the engravers.'

In September I went up to Straloch to pass the proofs with Kenneth Macleod. We sat on the steps of his church in the sunshine and passed page after page. He was for putting in anonymously the beautiful little tales and legends such as 'The Christ Child's Lullaby' or 'The Sealwoman's Croon', but I insisted that they should be signed, and as he would not do this himself I wrote the name, Kenneth Macleod, at the bottom of each already engraved page.

Before any of these appeared in print, there were two who valued them highly. One, my brother, Dr. Charles Kennedy, who had a quite uncanny sense of the exquisite and genuine in art, and who said that this prose of Kenneth Macleod would live even though the rest of the volume should become obsolete. The other, Wilfrid Gibson, the poet of 'Fires', 'Daily Bread', etc., whom I met first in 1908, at Jane Hay's, St. Abb's Haven. On hearing me speak the 'Christ Child's Lullaby', his ears flamed red with excitement. I have spoken that little prose tale in every corner of England and Scotland, in the capitals of France, Holland, German, Czechoslovakia, and Austria, and over a good part of America, and it never grows stale.

Part IV

FRUITION

Left: Patuffa Kennedy-Fraser

Right: Marjory
Kennedy-Fraser.
(Courtesy of Mrs.
Catriona Westland).

24

My First Volume.
London Recitals (1909)

The long-worked-on first volume of *Songs of the Hebrides* came out at last in May 1909, and we gave two recitals in the Steinway Hall, London (now the Grotrian), to introduce it. I was assisted by Margaret, Mrs. Matthay, and our youngest brother, John. Mrs. Matthay was already well known in London as speaker and singer of verse and ancient minstrelsie. John Kennedy had but recently settled there. Originally trained and having practised as a lawyer in Edinburgh, he finally adopted music as a profession, and his brochure *Common Sense in Singing,* published by Ricordi, was most highly thought of by Tobias Matthay (whose famous work on pianoforte playing, by the way, was also later characterized by Sir Hugh Allen of the Royal College of Music as just common sense). On hearing our two recitals, the London critics instantly recognized the freshness, beauty, and strength of this ancient melodic art, but some seemed surprised and puzzled that it should take so kindly to modern[1] treatment. May not the solution possibly be that some modern music had already been leavened by it? Ancient sea-faring songs like 'Kishmul's Galley', are they not akin to the melodic formulae used by Wagner after his epoch-making experience of northern sea-faring song, voyaging for three weeks in a small sailing vessel in the Baltic and about the shores of Norway? And my own experience of being soaked from childhood in ancient Scots tonality and yet enjoying a fairly wide

[1] In the sense that harmonic music since 1600 is modern.

137

culture in modern European harmonic music—may not these help to account for it?

Those first recitals in London were given on a Friday evening and Saturday afternoon. On the Monday, before leaving, I was invited to one of W. B. Yeats's regular gatherings of poets, etc. In a letter to Patuffa from Edinburgh on my return, I wrote:

On Monday night I drove to Euston, and without leaving the cab gave my luggage in charge of the porter at the station and drove on to Yeats's house. I bade the porter label baggage Edinburgh and that I should return at 11 o'clock. Cabby had some difficulty in finding 'Woburn Buildings', where the poet lived, but dropped me at last at the entrance to a very clean little lane just beside St. Pancras Church. It was paved with flagstones, so one could not drive up. I alighted and wandered down, looking for 18. I came upon a cobbler's window and just beside it, on a little worm-eaten doorway, I saw a bell. I rang timidly, and by and by heard a foot within descending the stairs. A young man opened for me, and I told him that Florence Farr was expecting me. I followed him up two narrow dark wooden ramshackle stairs, and was met on the landing by Yeats himself. He was most genial, and introduced me to a cosy little garret lit with the soft light of candles. . . He asked me all sorts of questions about the Hebrides and the singing of the folk. Shortly after, Lady Gregory came in and I had a long chat with her—a quiet, thin, practical, not at all ecstatic-looking woman. I sang them the 'Love Wandering' and the 'Sealwoman', and Florence Farr sang to the psaltery, and Yeats read a poem by Sturge Moore, who was there with his wife. . . I was sorry to tear myself away, but some minutes before 11, I got into my wraps and Yeats himself showed me down the rickety stairs. As I tucked up my long skirts, he and Florence Farr wondered how I was going to face Edinburgh in the morning in my evening-dress-hatless condition. I explained that I had planned to appear decent in the cold light of morning and of Edinburgh. When my cab arrived at Euston, there was my porter, and my bags were already in their place. One lady only was in the compartment with me, so I asked her to help me. We pulled down the blind, and I was already 'clothed and in my right mind' before the journey began. A Pullman sleeper has its points, but it's not so exciting. And when you indulge in the luxury of recitals in London you must economize in some fashion.

Our joy at the success of those first London recitals was overshadowed by the family loss that followed. We had been home again hardly a week when our brother Dr. Charles died suddenly of heart failure in his 50th year. A medical man, in private practice in Edinburgh, he was much loved by his patients. He was at the same time a born artist, a man of intellectual finesse and sympathetic insight. I missed him sorely. He was my reader of anything new. I have known him to read through at first sight one of the elusive songs of the modern French school, looking over my shoulder at the copy; then, freeing himself entirely from the notation, stand perhaps before the fireplace and repeat the whole song there and then from memory. But better than this, better than any mere note-perfect reading, his rendering of the new song was also as a rule (and this is much rarer) mood-perfect. He sang for me once the last four songs of the *Winterreise* at a Schubert lecture-recital. To those who heard it, it was an unforgettable interpretation. His was a beautiful character, unselfish, noble, loving, simple in manner, an artist in his inmost soul.

At that time, twenty-five years ago now, the English translations of Schubert's songs were mostly very poor—literal possibly, but prosaic, unmusical, unsingable. He fashioned singing versions for his own use, of which I give here these four.

Schubert's *Winterreise* (Winter's Journey)
(The last four songs)
Dr. Charles Kennedy's singing version of translation:

1. *DAS WIRTHSHAUS* = THE INN

A lonely churchyard greets me, and draws me to its side.
Ah, here may I find shelter, Ah, here may I abide!
Ye mounds with grass grown over, ye flowers and gardens green,
Ye surely are the tokens that welcome guests have been.

Is every chamber taken? Is there no place even here
For me, so faint and weary, for me, so lone and drear?
Cold-hearted Inn that opens not its doors on my behalf,
Then onward, ever onward, I and my trusty staff.

2. *MUTH* = COURAGE

Drives the snow upon my cheek; Shake it off like powder!
Would my heart within me speak? Sing I loud and louder.
Hearken not to its deep sobs, Have no ears for moaning;

Do not feel its bitter throbs, Fools are fond of groaning.
Bravely on our journey go, 'Gainst the storm we're driving;
Is no God on earth below? We ourselves are striving.

3. *DIE NEBENSONNEN* = THE MOCK SUNS

Three suns I saw shine in Heaven so bright,
I held them long and fast in sight,
And there they stand and burn so clear
As though they wished to hold me near.

Ah, ye three suns have here no place;
Your beams light up another face.
But side by side ye shone all three,
The best two now are gone from me!
Went first the sun those twain to leave
In darkness would I gladly grieve.

4. *DER LEIERMANN* = THE ORGAN-GRINDER

Up behind the village stands an organ man,
And with frozen fingers grinds as best he can,
Barefoot on the cold ground sways he to and fro
And his penny platter does not overflow.

No one seems to hear him, no one for him feels,
And the village dogs are snarling at his heels,
But he takes no thought of them or anything,
Grinds his hurdy-gurdy with the same old swing.

Good old organ-grinder, must you grind alone?
Won't your hurdy-gurdy to my ditty drone?

25

Barra Again.
A Waulking. Benbecula.
A Bridal Procession   (1911)

In the spring of 1911 the Government very kindly recognized the value of the Hebridean research work and awarded me a Civil List pension.[1] For a year or two after getting out my volume, I suffered from the effects of the overstrain, and while carrying on my ordinary professional work was not fit for anything further.

Yet the glamour of the Western sea, the lure of the Isles, and the snare of the elusive song-quest, these have drawn us time and again into their charmed circle. So it happened that summer after summer found us crossing the Minch to those 'out isles of the sea'.

In 1911, with Patuffa and her Auntie Jessie, (Mrs. Matthay), I visited Iona, Barra, and Benbecula. Iona, most beautiful and attractive of isles, is yet too far removed from the old order of things to yield much ancient music-lore. So we spent a delightful week-end there, and then crossed to Castle Bay.

From the church on the hill we looked down on Kishmul Castle, afloat on the waters of the Bay, built as it is on a rock that is covered at high tide. As the moving waters hypnotized us, we seemed to see, as three hundred years ago, the singer 'gazing seaward, watching Kishmul's galley sailing', as it

---

[1] In 1924 the Government again put its mark of approval on me and my research work by conferring on me the distinction of Commander of the Order of the British Empire.

'battled, without anchor, cable, or tackle, 'gainst the hurtling waves'. And as we looked, we saw at length the vessel miraculously at anchor by the Castle walls. And we heard again the strains of harping, 'sweet harping too', issuing from the narrow slits that served for windows in the fortresses of those old, unhappy, far-off days.

When we had had our fill of Castle Bay, we drove round to the west side of the island by the quaint hamlets of Kentangaval and Borve.

These still held fast (as did Eriskay) to the very ancient traditional form of house, nowhere now to be found on the mainland nor indeed in the Inner Isles. In the museum at Campbelltown, Kintyre, I remember being shown a model of an old island cottage and being astonished to find that it in no way approached the primitive type of the genuine Outer Island dwelling—was indeed on an entirely different plan.

Sir Leslie Mackenzie, who has toured the Isles on various health commissions, explains the so-called Black House as a most ingenious device on the part of the early isleman to render possible human and even animal life on those inhospital, windswept, rocky shores. I myself was lucky enough once in South Uist to see the process of evolving one of those dwellings out of the raw materials lying immediately to hand. Needless to say there was no hired labour on the job—no masons, no joiners. Each man just did his bit. On a great grey boulder, on the shore of South Uist, they erected a cone of dry peats, set fire to it, and there left it to smoulder overnight. Next day, buckets of cold sea-water were fetched from the shore and splashed against the rock, splitting it into irregular fragments. These were built into a rough wall enclosing an oval-shaped area, the wall very low (some three to four feet) and very thick (from five to eight feet). Half-way through its great thickness this dry-stane dyke was interlined with a layer of turf. As there are no trees on the islands, driftwood from across the Atlantic, gathered on the western shores of the islands, served as rafters and roofpoles, these resting, not on the outer edge of the wall, but half-way in, leaving two and a half feet or more of projecting wall. The roof frame, covered with turf and fern and bent grass *(muran)*, was fastened down finally by homemade ropes of heather, these weighted by big stones.

Now this projecting low wall served various purposes. Firstly, it protected the roof from the wind. The more violently the wind might blow against the low projecting wall, the more firmly the roof would settle into its place. Secondly, the wall formed at certain times a useful platform. In the middle of the rock floor of the interior of the cottage a peat fire was kept burning day and night. The smoke from this burning peat was allowed to permeate the thatch of the roof, and thus convert it into precious manure. This smoke-laden thatch had to be removed at regular intervals and replaced by fresh turf. The low projecting wall then served as a platform from which to work at the needful dismantling and re-thatching of the cottage roof. But the low wall served also at the Christmas and Hogmanay[1] Festivals. The boys of the township were wont then, as part of some ancient pageant, to encircle the house and sing some such *duan* to the houseman and the housewife as Duncan of the Sgeulach-dan in Eriskay sang to us and we recorded in our first volume:

> Heire bannock, Hoire bannock!
> Telling us that Christ was born,
> King of Kings and Lord of Lords,
> Son of Dawn, Son of Cloud,
> Son of Planets, Son of Stars,
> Son of Rivers, Son of Dew,
> Son of Welkin, Son of Sky.

These were evidently survivals of ancient heathen rites converted to Christian uses. The Christmas boys went robed in white.

Of the Hogmanay doings, Dr. Alexander Carmichael in his *Carmina* tells how the leader of the band would be robed in the hard hide of a bull, with the horns and hoof still adhering. Arrived at the house, the lads would leap up on to the low

---

[1]Scots last day of the year.

projecting wall and run round it sunwise, the 'hide'-man shaking his horns and hoofs, the others striking him with sticks, the while they sang:

> I am come to your country
> To renew the Hogmanay,
> As it was in the time of our forefathers.
> I ascend by the door lintel,
> I descend by the doorstep[1]

Carmichael suggests that this rite may have been symbolic of the laying of an evil spirit.

There were no right angles in the walls of the ancient cottages; no gables, the walls being of uniform height throughout; and no chimneys. The smoke was too valuable an agricultural asset to be allowed to escape scot-free!

The area covered by the roof sufficed to accommodate not only the folk but also the cattle, and the heated interiors served to keep the beasts alive, on very little food, during the winter months.

The spring was the tragic time, when food supplies were apt to run short. Father Allan told me that in Eriskay, at times, man and beast alike were reduced to living on seafare.

Well, in 1911 Kentangaval and Borve in Barra were—and still are to a large extent—hamlets of just such strange, yet cosy and picturesque dwellings, and into these cottages Mrs. Matthay, Patuffa, and I entered (with a message always from Annie Johnson) to gather songs.

In one we found an old dame, Ishbel Macneill, a direct descendant of the pirate chiefs of Barra.

Seated in the dark interior of her little cottage, her head bound in a cashmere shawl of ivory and arab red, she had a far-away look in her eyes and a waxen smoothness, as of death, on her finely chiselled features. Beyond our reach she seemed, but on our crooning to her an old song she was recalled to life

---

[1] See *Carmina Gadelica,* volume 1.

144

and her mind again leapt out to the life behind her. When we reluctantly bade her good-bye, she was still excitedly crooning to herself.

The chief event of our short stay in the Isle was a waulking, got up for our benefit by Annie Johnson's mother. The woollen web to be shrunk was some blanketing she had herself spun. We were leaving for Benbecula next day, so the waulking had to take place in the middle of the week.

The waulking songs are probably the oldest among the surviving songs of the Isles. Unlike spinning, which may be performed either alone or in company, waulking calls for the collaboration of from ten to twenty women. The songs used are evolved from the rhythm of this communal labour, unfamiliar now on the mainland and fast passing away even from the Isles. This shrinking of the home-spun, home-woven web was done by the process of soaking it in dilute ammonia, then thumping it long and vigorously on an improvised table until it dried. Communal labour tends to conserve the chants used in its practice, and in waulking the heavy, long-sustained, steadily rhythmical work could only be performed with the help of such strongly rhythmical song. And if waulking is the most important of communal labour-song functions, it is also the gayest. Its gaiety is infectious, as any one who has had the good fortune to assist at a waulking can testify. Little wonder the old wives tell that when they were girls it was held a greater privilege to be invited to a waulking than even to a dance! At a waulking the young men take no active part, they look on from a respectful distance by the open door or skylight window of the barn where the women, young and old, are seated at work. No doubt the lads make note the while of the particular maiden they hope to see home after the function, but the onlookers here are not essential. The real source of joy for the women lies in the strangely exhilarating effect of socially performed, long-continued repetitions of any bodily movements accompanied by song.

At this waulking we were women only: the men were out with the boats, and the women were already tired with a hard day's herring-packing. Yet the stirring old waulking song dispelled weariness and stimulated even the aged leaders to long-sustained exertion.[1] At waulkings and social functions of any kind it is the custom to leave the door open and to welcome any one who cares to enter. While we were in the thick of the excitement in Mrs. Johnson's barn—all the lookers-on joining in the exhilarating refrains—a woman entered, dressed entirely in black, with black draperies over her head. She came slowly in, and after a while glided as slowly out. It had a strange effect, this 'skeleton at the feast', but no one disturbed her.

A long narrow table had been improvised in the candle-lit barn. The women were seated on benches on either side. At one end stood a wooden tub in which the blanket was soaking. From the tub it was lifted and gathered in the hand like a thick woollen scarf, then stretched down the table to the far end, where, turned back on itself, it lay along the boards like an elongated letter 'C'.

The seated women, grasping in both hands the portion of thick scarf which lay before them, lifted it and began slowly to beat it rhythmically on the boards, the two sides alternating in movement.

An old woman, one of the two song-leaders, began to croon softly. And, as one listened, a quaint refrain shaped itself, a theme fashioned in strong rhythmic and melodic outlines, calculated, like a fuge subject, to impress itself easily on the memory. This was caught up and repeated by the workers *tutti*. A verse-phrase of a recitative-like character, perhaps consisting of only eight notes to eight syllables, was then intoned by the leader; and this was followed by a second refrain, longer than the first, but again of a strongly rhythmical character. This, in its turn, was caught up and repeated in chorus. And now the leader sang the alternating verse portions only, leaving the

[1] We left the island next day, but heard that one of these, a very frail little old woman, had to be kept in bed for three weeks to recover.

refrains to the other women. But the musical interest was not yet exhausted, for the leader skilfully varied the verse themes, and I tried in vain to catch and note all the changes rung on a few notes by one of these capable, practised folksingers of the Isles.

As the workers got heated with the excitement of tone and rhythm and carried away by the hypnotic effect of repetition, the work became more and more rapid, and the cloth passed gradually round the table sun-wise. The possibilities of one song having been exhausted, a second was intoned by a fresh leader, who in her turn set the pattern of the refrain or refrains (some songs have only one recurrent refrain), and exercised her skill also in the improvisation of verse strains.

And when, after many songs, the waulking proper came to an end, the web was carefully rolled up and clapped. And the humorous 'Bodachan' was the clapping-song we heard that night.

Despite the delicious sadness which is said to prevail in Celtic song, we find humorous songs galore, dealing with the doings of houseman and housewife, after the fashion of the classic Lowland songs 'Tak' Your Auld Cloak Aboot Ye' and 'Get up and Bar the Door'. This Barra song telling of a Bottachan, who coming home hungry and angry to a supperless house crunches the great grey quernstanes[1] in his wrath, finds a parallel in Breton song. There, a woman finding herself in a like quandary to that of the unprepared gudewife of the Isles confesses to us her plight, since the grain is still to reap, the butter is still in the market, etc.

> Mon mari m'a commandé
> Des crêpes pour son dîner.
> Mais comment le contenter, commère?
> La poêle est chez l'chaudronnier,
> La farine à récolter,
> Et le beurre est au marché, commère.

[1]The stones of the ancient primitive handmill or quern.

BENBECULA. A BRIDAL PROCESSION

We left Barra next day for Benbecula. To reach it we had to land from the little steamer at Lochboisdale in South Uist and drive northwards the length of the island through bog-land, lower at times than sea-level, lit slantwise by the afternoon sun glinting on long chains of water-lily lochs. We drove past the farm where Flora Macdonald was born and came at nightfall to one of the dangerous sea fords that serve to cut off the Isle of Benbecula from the outside world.[1]

It was at this ford that Flora was held up for the night, when on her way to Clanranald's place to contrive the serving-woman's disguise in which she conveyed Bonnie Prince Charlie to her mother's home in Skye. And we too were held up, but only by the tide.

Driving across the ford early next morning, we had to tramp five miles (and a bittock) in drenching rain and driving wind to the cosy fireside of a crofter, Calum Barraich, the last apparently of the race of Ossianic singers, a type even then supposed to have long since passed away.

A pastoral people are the folk of Benbecula, the surrounding sea too shallow for fishing-craft. Calum had spent over seventy years herding cattle on the grassy flats of the Machair, which stretches its white sands westward to the Atlantic. I had been attracted to the Isle by the fame of Calum as a singer of sacred songs. I looked for incantations and hymns such as are the staple of Carmichael's *Carmina Gadelica*. What was my astonishment to find that Calum's repertoire consisted entirely of ancient, rhymed, heroic tales and songs of pagan origin, just such Ossianic fragments indeed as Macpherson found here in the eighteenth century when covering this selfsame gound in search of materials for his famous epic. When Macpherson's English interconnected version of this fugitive, fragmentary, orally transmitted lore appeared, all Europe reverberated to his Ossian. Macpherson died in 1796, but long before his death his

---

[1]These tidal fords are very dangerous, the one that separates Benbecula from North Uist being five miles across.

poems, founded on these fragments, had become, according to William Sharp, one of the most vital influences in literature.

To Calum therefore we went. At eighty-seven, still bright and active, he was to be seen daily out on the Machair herding his cattle. And in the clean white-sanded kitchen of his thatched cottage he sang, but not before he had set everything in perfect order for the ceremony—these old pagan tales were sacred to the Isleman. In a corner of the kitchen stood the hand-loom on which was stretched a blanket in the course of weaving; by the fire sat the *cailleach* carding or combing out wool; by the door a young woman spinning; and by the other side of the fire the old, keen, bright-eyed, white-haired keeper of the traditional lore himself.

He chanted many lays, some on a monotone, the phrases defined by cadences, some on a gradually descending scale within the compass of a sixth, and among them a well-defined air to which he sang the lay of Aillte.

AILLTE[1]

The Queen of Lochlin of the brown shields,
Deep love gave, that all endureth,
To Aillte young, of the keen-edge blades,
And secretly with him fled she.

The King of Lochlin, his hardy hosts
In this hour of need gathered,
And with them came the mighty stalwarts
Of nine kings from the northern shores.

There were that wounded fell,
Or died on the field of battle,
But never one was home returning,
Of all the mighty Lochlin men.

Aillte, the hero of the lay, one of the handsomest of the young stalwarts of the Fayne, hurt that his leader, Fionn, had not included him among those bidden to a feast, fled to the court of the King of Lochlin and to him offered his services for a year and a day. The Queen, like another Helen, took the love of her heart for the young Gael, and together they escaped and sought the protection of the Fayne.

[1]Pronounce like the English words, *isle-char.*

149

The King of Lochlin, enraged at the rape of the Queen, gathered his hosts and the hosts of nine other kings and descended on Fionn and the Fayne.

And as the old Benbecula singer chanted the last verses, that tell of the glories of the Gael, his body became tense with excitement and his eyes glowed with the fire of racial memory.

A strange, remote island is Benbecula, more cut off by its fords perhaps than even Eriskay by its currents. Low lying, watery, its atmospheric conditions are favourable to optical illusions. The farther away an object stands the larger it looms on the horizon. I remember my first day there starting gaily off to walk to a house that seemed near, and how I nearly cried with vexation when I found that the nearer I approached it the farther it seemed to draw away. Indeed, a fellow-traveller afterwards related to me how she had seen there one day what she took at first to be a mirage. It was a grove of trees on the horizon. Now there are no trees on those wind-swept isles. So she made towards the vision and kept it in sight. The trees gradually diminished to the height of a hedgerow and in the end proved to be a row of potato shaws!

In the chapel that stood on the western sands, just beside Calum's croft, we assisted at an island wedding. After the ceremony the bridal party formed up, with a piper at their head, to cut slantwise across the Machair to the bridegroom's house, some five miles distant. As we returned, driving by the high road, we could follow the progress of the party in the gathering darkness not alone by the music of the bagpipes but also by the sound of gunshots fired from each lamp-lit thatched cottage, as the bridal party approached and passed. The moon hung like a lamp from the dome of heaven, and the heat of the long summer day was raising white bridal veils of mist from each of the thousand and one little tarns and lochans that dispute the land in Benbecula. The bride must have been very tired at the end of it all. After the five-mile walk to her new home they danced, so we were told, to the sound of the pipes and the laughter of the sea until the 'sma' 'oors' of the morning.

150

26

Eigg (1912)

In the spring of 1912 we had arranged to give a Hebridean recital in the Bechstein Hall, London (now the Wigmore); the singers—Margaret, myself, Mrs. Matthay, and John. Two or three days before the recital date, as John was travelling to Bristol to give some lessons there, he was seized with terrible pain while in the railway carriage, and after an operation on arrival died from heart failure at the age of 45. We were present at his cremation at Golders Green on the very date of the proposed Hebridean recital. An impressive performance of numbers from Brahms's *Requiem* was carried through by his friend Ernest Reade. We carried the urn with us to Edinburgh, and laid his ashes with those of his father and mother in the Grange Cemetery.

That summer and again in 1913 I persuaded Kenneth Macleod to come with me to his own native isle, Eigg. He had not revisited it, I learned afterwards, for over twenty years, and had feared that by doing so he might lose the glamorous memories of his youth. When confessing this to me, we sat long gazing over from Laig Bay to the 'altar isle of the sea', the Isle of Rhum. 'But even after seeing the Bay of Naples', he continued, 'I think Eigg and Rhum more beautiful than ever.'

In Eigg Kenneth Macleod was born, and there cradled in Celtic lore. He had had for a nurse a singer reputed the best in the island, and his aunt Janet Macleod from Skye was one of the hereditary conservers of the traditions of the Macleods.

These gifted women found a receptive and retentive mind in young Kenneth. At the age of thirteen, influenced by MacBain of Inverness Academy, he became a conscious collector, much of what he gathered into the honey-cells of his memory being deposited finally in our joint volumes of Hebridean songs. In Eigg, with him, I had an easy task as collector—merely to appreciate, phonograph, and notate the material he brought to light. The old people, who all knew and loved him, not only gave him freely what they could recall, but now from himself they heard so many half-forgotten lines and quaint tunes and refrains that from the deeply disturbed depths of their minds, stirred in the old lore as they had not been for many a day, songs and tales re-emerged that neither they nor their neighbours had thought of for years. And thus, besides the lilts and croons of everyday work-a-day life, we found still alive among them fragmentary, pre-Christian, heroic lore. Such were the tales and songs of Cuchullan, the sun-god and fighting hero (already becoming obsolete in the days of Columba), and that of Parsifal or the *Amadan Mor.*

On our second visit, in 1913, we took a gay little company of music-makers on holiday with us from London, including Professor and Mrs. Matthay and Mr. Matthay's pupil Myra Hess, the famous pianist. Kenneth Macleod on that occasion christened Matthay 'the Wizard', because out of a bag he had brought with him seemed to come, at need, every device of civilization. Fortunately he had among these a camera, which got one or two good snapshots of the Isle and the folk. I never could carry a camera: a graphophone, inclined to go out of order, and a set of blank records was enough on my mind!

It was a rare treat for all to visit the legend-rich wells and caves with Kenneth, and wander among its hazel woods and over its peaty moorland listening to his old-world lore. I was very anxious about the weather, for it is sometimes so stormy as to make it impossible to land or to leave Eigg's shores. But Providence was kind, and the folk from the South came and left in calm and sunshine.

152

27

Visits to America   (1913-16)

Towards the end of 1913 there came an invitation from the MacDowell Society of New York to go out there and give a recital of our Hebridean songs. They fixed 2 December as the date, and we had but a fortnight to prepare for the trip. I took Patuffa with me—Margaret did not care to go. Patuffa had been studying singing for some years with Margaret and had made a few tentative appearances, so I decided to take her, mainly as accompanist. We could spare only six weeks, and as three of these were spent on the Atlantic going and coming we had but three weeks on the other side.

The MacDowell Club room, used both as a picture gallery and a concert room, seemed to me a trifle too intimate. For although our work may seem intimate, I always feel more at home on a platform that detaches me somewhat from my audience. Not only does one gain in artistic freedom in this, but the Hebridean songs, most of them, suggest great spaces. A song like 'Caristiona', for instance, I can hardly sense at all in the confined space of a small room.

After New York we sang at Princeton University, where I was mightily flattered to be told that I recalled Ellen Terry, who had been giving an afternoon there but a short time before. We sang also at Cornell, where my son was Assistant Professor in Educational Psychology, and where we had a truly cosmopolitan audience. I must confess I felt somewhat staggered when first I stepped on the platform there and saw so many Orientals

153

in the audience. But I soon learned to have no qualms as to the possible response to our songs, whatever the components of our audience. The rhythm of Hebridean melody apparently reaches and touches the hearer, whatever the race or colour.

We gave a recital in Boston, *en route* for Halifax, whence we sailed. I thus renewed acquaintance with Nova Scotia after thirty years. There had been a great migration of Hebrideans at one time to Nova Scotia. The nature of the land and water as one approaches Halifax is strangely akin to that described by Renan as characteristic of Brittany—and truly characteristic also of the Hebridean Isles. While there, we stayed with my sister Helen and her husband, George S. Campbell. In the town we gave a Hebridean recital for the funds of Dalhousie College, and thence sailed again for home.

A second invitation came from America in 1916, and Patuffa and I again toured there, going as far west as Chicago.

On the second tour Patuffa appeared as harpist and as singer also to her own harp accompaniment. Her small Celtic harp, a modern reproduction of the ancient bardic instrument, had been made for her by Morley in London. It is a trying instrument to keep fit in sudden changes of temperature. Frequently, in the over-heated rooms in the States, a string would break while we were in the middle of a recital. While she was replacing it beside me on the platform, I was wont to elaborate a little more the introduction to a song or to give heaped-up measure to a description of the Isles until she was ready again.

At our recital in the Aeolian Hall in New York we were lucky in that we had the presence and the warm appreciation of the then still living *doyen* of New York musical critics, Krehbiel. He had been already a critic in New York fifty years before, when my father first sang there in 1867, and he now welcomed me as my father's daughter. One of the New York exclusive musical people remarked to me that Krehbiel was surely quite dotty over me. But it touched me very much that he had been the same over my father, and now turned the full flood of his enthusiasm on me and on my work and on Patuffa's minstrelsy. Another

154

notable among the audience was Padraic Colum, the Irish poet. We felt him there as a shining spirit.

We had many good friends in New York. We met singers and players galore at the house of Frances Emilie Bauer, the foremost woman music critic in the city; we were entertained as distinguished foreign guests at several of the formal public breakfasts,[1] a feature of New York intellectual life; and we were motored out to lovely country houses, where we breathed freely after the weeks of imprisonment in that region of sky-scrapers.

We had wonderful audiences and still more wonderful hospitality. It is reported than Masefield, as a guest at one of the New York literary breakfasts, was heard to say: 'As for American hospitality, it is cut in chunks'. Certainly it was cut in chunks for Patuffa and me. In Chicago Mrs. Vaughn Moody, the poet-dramatist's widow, took us under her wing and housed us in the rooms in which she lodged in succession Tagore, Masefield, John Drinkwater, Wilfrid Gibson, and others. At her home we met famous American littérateurs and artists: among them the Chicago-ites, Lee Masters and Carl Sandberg. In place of the formal dinner, she every evening had supper served in her dimly lit library on small tables, which appeared from nowhere and were set before each guest, as he or she appeared, and removed again as quietly when a guest, for some other engagement, had to leave. Thus she surrounded herself with the society of artists and gave pleasure to others as well as to herself.

When the warm weather came, she carried us east to her farm in New England. Her summer house was a romantically conceived log-cabin with an open verandah built on the steep slope of a wooded hill-side, the verandah on which we sat seeming to seeming to rest, Peter-Pan-wise, among the branches of a great tree as it swung over the valley below.

While there, Patuffa went over to the Rip Van Winkle country, to sit for her portrait with the harp to the well-known American portrait-painter Orlando Rowlands.

---

[1] We were guests of honour one morning at Ely's Literary Luncheon, and met there Vachell Lindsay, the famous tramp poet.

It came about this way. In New York we had many letters of introduction. One we could not use until the day before leaving the city for Chicago. We had been giving an afternoon recital to the Biennial Congress of Women's Clubs. Patuffa was in her medieval harping dress. We drove straight to Orlando Rowlands' studio—it was their day at home—to present the letter of introduction. As we entered, the painter and his charming wife exchanged glances. He had been raving to her all winter about the vision of a harpist whom he was to paint. Patuffa materialized that vision.

We were arranging to stay on in the States and had engagements for Cincinnati, Chicago, etc., when we were suddenly cabled to return home.

28

London Recitals.
The Seal-woman Opera (1917)

Early in 1917 Patuffa joined one of Lena Ashwell's war concert parties, and sang the Hebridean songs to her harp in France. There were many Orientals in her audiences, and they delighted in some of the songs, recognizing the affinity between the ancient island hypnotic croons and their own old world traditional airs.

In March of that year Patuffa, having returned from France, joined me in recitals at the Aeolian Hall. This was her first appearance in London, and we met with such success that we have continued the London recitals ever since. Every season we have endeavoured to introduce fresh programmes of the material recovered. For some six years we confined our recitals to the Chamber Music Hall (the Aeolian), but in the end had to move to the large Queen's Hall to accommodate our audiences. What a world of friendship and loving appreciation the publications and the recitals opened up! I have hardly been able to draw breath in the last ten years, I have had so many kind letters, so many appreciations, so many inquiries about the songs, so many engagements to give recitals all over England and Scotland.

In June 1917, after our first recital at Aeolian Hall, Professor Granville Bantock invited us to give a programme at Birmingham University. We had a crowded room in the University Hall. Ernest Newman, the famous critic, was there. Two nights later, we gave a second recital in Sir Barry Jackson's little theatre. Newman was again present. The following day he wrote an

157

appreciation in the *Birmingham Post,* which in my most enthusiastic moments I could not have surpassed. It ran:

> Mrs. Kennedy-Fraser holds the highest place among British folksong collectors. She has a poet's love of the islands and the peculiar phase of civilization they represent: also a very skilled musician, the accompaniments are equal to the best that has been done in any other field. There are melodies among these songs that are as purely perfect as any melody could be. Schubert and Hugo Wolf would have knelt and kissed the hands of the men who conceived them . . . Schubert himself never wrote a more perfectly satisfying or more haunting melody than that of the 'Seagull of the Land-under-Waves'.

What touched me most in this appreciation was that I myself had gone out to the Isles, straight from intensive private study and public lecturing on those two greatest of song-writers, and had come myself to much the same conclusion as to the relative values of the melodic material. I had so learned to dissociate vocal melody from pianoforte framework (in my lectures) that I was ready now to recognize the value of this stark, strong, Hebridean stuff—a value which, in some cases, might otherwise have escaped me.

Some weeks of that summer Patuffa and I spent at Harlech in Wales, where were also Bantock, Cyril Scott, and Joseph Holbrooke. I went because Bantock had suggested my writing him a libretto for a proposed opera on the Hebridean legend of 'The Seal-woman'. The libretto was soon written, and the musical side of it went gaily forward for a time, until it stuck for some years. Just then the long delayed volume 2 of *Songs of the Hebrides* at last came from the press, and I was able to hand a still unbound copy to Bantock in Harlech. For long he kept the two volumes lying side by side on his desk.

We were a happy group at Harlech. Alfred Perceval Graves entertained us in his castle there. Cyril Scott was a strange, aloof member of the party. He reminded me of a tensely strung, nervous, high-bred horse. Joseph Holbrooke was quite different. He played us some weird and wonderful variations of his own on Scots airs. Of the Hebridean melodies, when asked how he liked them, all he had to say was that 'the old Scots songs were good enough for him'.

The opera finally came to a hearing in the autumn of 1924, and we gave fourteen consecutive performances of it in Sir Barry Jackson's theatre, Birmingham. Sir Barry asked me to undertake the part of the old crone, Mary Macleod, the famous old Hebridean song-maker of three hundred years ago.

It was a reckless undertaking at my age. I had certainly studied for opera in Italy in my young days, but had never thought of going on the stage. And fourteen consecutive performances —every night of the week and one matinée weekly! I throve on it, nevertheless, although I was suffering all through with a touch of influenza. But I was petted and mothered by my kind friends the Schurhoffs, with whom I stayed. Stage work, in a way, I found easier than that of the concert platform. So much of the atmosphere is provided for you by costume, scenery, and a *throughout* story or plot.

The opera has since been heard on the wireless—I took part in that performance also, and the lovely orchestral texture of the sea-music (Bantock is a superb orchestral tone-colour painter of the sea) suffers naught from being divorced from stage setting. Indeed, the whole story of such an opera may be well left to the imagination.

Adrian Boult was our conductor, and entered alike into the spirit of the songs (there are sixteen Hebridean songs incorporated in the work) and into that of the beautiful orchestral framework. Among our audience we had on two occasions Laura Knight, the famous painter and the first woman R.S.A., who greatly enjoyed the fierce *puirt a beul* (mouth tune) 'Mac il ioro', which I give to the old crone to sing to the fishers. Paul Shelving was our scenic artist, and he built up a strange Fingal's-cave-like structure of rocks, up and down which I was apt to run too swiftly, Sir Barry thought, for the old dame I was impersonating!

29

The Lewes and Skye   (1919-22)

During the war years no one might cross the Minch save only those compelled to do so either by duty or kinship. But in 1919 we were able to resume our visits to the Isles. In that year Patuffa and I, and in 1920[1] Margaret and I, were guests of Lord Leverhulme at Stornoway Castle in the Lewes. Our host generously put every means at our disposal to get over the big area of the Lewes on our song-research.

One day, in search of songs, Margaret and I ventured from Garry-na-hine on the west coast, in a converted motor-boat, through Loch Roag to Bernera, William Black's 'Thule'. 'Such a boat!' writes Margaret. 'It was like a small barge, roofed over. We sat on the roof, and as the sides sloped down to the sea you can imagine what we felt like when the boat rolled. And worse still, we seemed to be heading for the Atlantic!'

We were to be landed at Tobson, a farm on the Isle. Lady Kathleen Lindsay, deputed chaperone on this occasion, had arranged the trip with the boatman who takes the mail over daily. She had asked him if it would be safe to go straight by boat to Tobson, where we were told we might get songs; as otherwise we would have a walk of three miles, landing at the usual stage. He said it might be possible if the weather was good. So we had at last what we thought was good weather, for the sun was shining. But we found when out in the channel that

---

[1] In 1920 Patuffa married the Rev. J. C. Fulton Hood, and ceased accompanying me on my song-research forays to the Isles, although she still collaborates with me in our Hebridean recitals.

this was a very risky expedition indeed. The farm people at Tobson, watching us from their windows, wondered what mad folk these were, coming straight towards them in that old hulk of a converted barge, instead of making for the normal landing-stage three miles distant. We landed, but had not been an hour on the Island, and I was just getting into the swing of an old song from a peat-carrier whom I found resting in the farm-kitchen, when our boatman came hurriedly and said, 'We must leave at once'. So we tumbled *on* to the boat again—I cannot say *in,* for the inserted motor occupied all the interior and we had to cling on for dear life to the wooden awning or roof, railingless, above. As we rolled back again through the churning channel, we learned to our amazement that our boatman in his long experience of crossing to the Isle had only once before risked going by that same route to that same landing-stage.

In Skye in 1922 and 1924 Margaret and I were the guests of Macleod of Skeabost and his lady. We found a number of enthusiastic young men singers there, who sang songs for our recording and who will doubtless do much to keep alive the traditional singing for well over another generation. We met also at Portree a rare old singer from South Harris, Lexie Macrae, from whom we noted the lovely 'Herding Prayer', the rousing 'Yont the Coolins' (a sail-hoisting chanty), the exhilarating 'Leaping Galley', and the yearning 'To the Isle of Skye'.

While there we visited Frances Tolmie in her own cottage at Dunvegan; we were entertained to tea by the Chief himself in the Castle, and sang the 'Fairy Lull-song' in the banqueting-room where is still preserved the silken flag which the fairy woman is said to have wrapped round the baby chief as she lulled him to sleep a thousand years ago.

One day we were driven by our hostess to the far north, to Kilmoluag, to shake hands with Mary Ross, from whom Frances Tolmie the aged singer had long before noted the lovely airs of 'The Seagull of the Land-under-Waves' and 'Caristiona'. While driving north we rested by a lonely Celtic cross, erected to the memory of Flora Macdonald, which looks westward across the Minch to South Uist, where the Jacobite heroine was born.

30

The Seal Song   (1920–7)

The Northern Isles did not yield us such a rich harvest of song
as did those farther to the west and south, possibly because
they were so much larger and thus more difficult to canvas. To
Barra, therefore, but twelve miles in circumference, we crossed
most frequently. I was there in the summer of 1920, and 1923.

I had the good fortune, guided again by my staunch friend
Annie Johnson, to find a fruitful source of still unnoted song in
the small, remote township of North Bay. The singer there,
whose wealth of song finally decided the need for further
publications, was a grandam known among the folk as 'Bean
Shomhairle Bhig', her formal title being Mrs. McKinnon.

North Bay was a good six-and-a-half to seven miles from our
head-quarters at Castle Bay, over the rocks by the east or
through the great stretches of sand by the west. In August 1923
Ruth Waddell, 'cellist, who was visiting the Isle, came with me
on my first visit, and we found the singer quietly seated in her
own cottage alone.

In a state of rare ecstatic musicalness she sang song after song
in such rapid succession that we could neither note nor remember any of them. So we had to turn homeward without any
record of our experience, and I vowed to get my graphophone
sent to me as soon as possible. On a second visit Annie Johnson
came with me, and she noted the words while I noted the tunes
with pencil and paper. Fortunately the graphophone arrived
just the day before I had to leave the island, and I started out
again for a third and last song-foray on North Bay.

We had ordered a two-wheeled trap to come for us; but, alas, it arrived late with two spokes run into the tire of a wheel. We had to go at snail's pace. I got a lift in a passing cart, but the cart turned in at Borve; and about half-way to North Bay a violent thunderstorm drove us into the maimed dog-cart, danger of a spill notwithstanding.

Our singer, forewarned, had her kitchen crowded this time with folk. Singing into the aluminium bell of a graphophone does not make for ecstatic performance, and the versions of the songs recorded were not on the whole as good as those already heard. But the records served their purpose. They substantiated the order of my notation, of which I had had some doubt.

It was now seven o'clock in the evening of a September day; and we had yet to do, on foot, in the dark, the six or seven miles that lay between us and our lair. The rain was falling in torrents: the wind blew 'as 'twere blawin' its last'. We left the graphophone, as it was heavy. We carried with us our precious records and breasted the hills that lay between us and light and fire and bed, and in speechless and dogged onward swing tramped our way home.

One other adventure in Barra at that time comes to mind. As I was walking back along the western shore from my second visit to the old singer at North Bay, I chanced on Ruth Waddell and her sister Maimie (violinist) as they rested on the sands in the warm afternoon sun. Glad of the rest, I lay down between them. We were some distance from the water's edge, parallel with which ran a long line of skerries, reefs that are covered at high tide. On the skerries lay basking in the sun a number of the great grey seals—seals that visit these isles only at intervals. My friends, great enthusiasts for the Hebridean songs—they use their own fine string-instrument arrangements for their students —said to me: 'Sing them the "Seal-woman's Sea Joy".'[1] In the great stretch of the four miles of white sands running north and south there was no sign of human presence, no movement save

[1] This was a song I had noted some twelve years earlier from an old South Uist woman who called it a seal song.

that of the seagulls. I raised myself only on my elbow—happily I did not show myself erect—and sang to this strange far-away audience the first phrase of the song. Instantly there was a response from the seal rocks. Like a fusillade, single note after single note came from each seal in succession from the southerly end of the reefs to the north.

Then, from out a few seconds of intense silence, came a beautiful solo voice which sang to us a phrase we had never heard before. I had my pencil and paper in hand on which I had been noting the songs of 'Bean Shomhairle Bhig'. I noted the seal air at once, and showing it to the 'cellist and violinist asked, 'Is that so?' and they answered, 'That is so'. The voice of the seal was so beautiful (of a rich mezzo-soprano quality) and the *cantabile* so perfect, that I should almost have believed I had been dreaming but for the corroboration of my two musician fellow-hearers. What did it mean? Did they take me for another seal?

Punch made some good fun of this when I related it to my London audience. The writer of the skit suggested that the British National Opera might retrieve its losses by capturing and exploiting that same seal prima donna!

I was in Barra last in August 1927. It still preserved its old character. The crofters, on the long summer days, carried home their peats in slow-moving carts or in creels on the flanks of the Barra ponies. The women with their pails went up the hill in the long summer evenings to milk the kye, and they dug too for cockles in the wonderful opalescent strand of Eoligarry. But there seemed now to be little spinning and no weaving.

That we and the young folk of the Isles themselves might hear some of the grand old labour-lilts connected with the cloth-weaving, sung in the old-time community fashion, we got up a great waulking. We held it in the school-house at North Bay. To be sure, we had to be content to function on imported blankets. But if there were no home-woven webs to shrink there were still, among the older women, some who were good at the songs, and that was the main thing. This cloth-shrinking festival is indeed fast becoming an almost forgotten rite, and great was the excitement of the community over the preparations for it.

The long refectory-like table with its attendant high forms running parallel down either side was fixed in the middle of the big school-room, while along the walls and on the floor in front was accommodation for a big audience, mostly young people of the Island who had never heard nor seen the like before.

Those women who still had the tradition were keen on the festival and came long distances to take part in it. There were so many experts gathered together that they vied with each other as to who should 'raise' the most uncommon song. Among the songs sung were some sad and soulful ones which suffered from being exploited thus for communal rhythm. But the excitement of the audience, the artificial light (they will not begin to waulk until night creeps in), the hypnotic rhythm of the swaying body and the cumulative effect of song upon song, each with an exciting refrain, brings out an exuberance, an *élan* that are hard to recapture when asking for the same songs in the sometimes dreary light of the next morning.

These refrain songs I find the most interesting quarry in the whole song-hunt. They are probably many centuries old, and make glorious community singing to-day just because they have stood the test of generations of use.

But life is rapidly changing, even in the Outer Isles, and there has probably been more change there in the last twenty years (I began research twenty-four years ago) than in the previous three hundred.

Before leaving the Isle I was seated one sunny morning in a sunny corner between the buttresses of the church on the hill that overlooks Kishmul Castle. Calum MacIain, sitting beside me, spoke of his father's days—how the men were wont always to intone a certain prayer for safety as they encircled their bark before leaving for a long voyage. He sang me the prayer and I wrote it down as he sang: 'But', he added, 'it was sung in my father's day for the last time'. None of the seamen who sang it that day ever returned. All were taken as toll by the sea.

31

Conclusion

In the intervening summers I had paid frequent visits to Kenneth Macleod in his own parish and noted something fresh every time, often from his elder sister Marion, now dead, who well remembered the old Eigg lore. It would come to her quite unexpectedly, and we never knew when she would recall fresh words and airs or perhaps merely refrains. Considerably older than her brother Kenneth, and having remained in the Isle for some time after he had left to pursue his school and university studies, she had had longer as well as earlier opportunities of acquiring the traditional lore.

In Colonsay, where he was pastor for five years, I noted from her the airs of 'Dance to Your Shadow', 'The Cockle Gatherer', 'Mac il ioro' (the fierce reiver *puirt-a-bial*), 'The Wind on the Moor', 'Putting Out to Sea', 'The Rune of the Weaver', and 'To People Who Have Gardens'. Later, in the Isle of Gigha, she sang me the fatalistic 'Sea-bird Flying Hither, Tell Me', one of the airs of 'Macleod's Galley', 'The Iona Rainbow', and the beautiful 'Eye of Springtide'.

The love for the songs of the Hebrides has spread all over England, and we have been invited to sing them in nearly all the cities and towns, big and small, north, west, south, and east. In Huddersfield, I remember, the British Music Society, as elsewhere, engaged us to give a recital. Next day the mayor of the town invited us to hear a massed singing of combined choirs from a number of the schools. Among their favourite songs, it appeared, was 'The Eriskay Love Lilt'. This they sang to me.

Thereupon Dr. Eaglefield Hull asked me to speak to the young people about the island whence the song came. I spoke to them enthusiastically about the small remote isles such as Mingulay and Eriskay. How the one type, that of Mingulay or St. Kilda, was little more than a jagged tooth of rock rising sheer out of the angry waters of the Atlantic, the people characterized by independence, gaiety, and strength. The other type, say Eriskay, lying more green and tranquil, great stretches of *Machair* (sandy dunes) and sheen-white sands 'reaching out to meet a shoaling sea, the lovely blues playing into the greens'. How the folk there were more tranquil, visionary, and resigned. And how, over all, jagged rock, green Machair, sheen-white sands, there broods ever an ineffable, spiritual beauty of space, colour, the infinite.

After my excursion into the island fairyland, the mayor addressed the young people; and said to them did they not feel glad that they lived in Huddersfield and not in those lonely Isles!

But who shall say? I have already told of a young man from St. Kilda (a suburb of Melbourne in Australia which was originally founded by colonists who went out there from the Hebridean St. Kilda) who paid a visit to his grandfather's native isle in the Hebrides. He came to see me afterwards, and told me that the strongest impression he had brought away with him after a month spent on that isle was one of the intense happiness of its people!

He spoke to me also of the hard conditions of life that had prevailed there until a hundred years ago. Life could be sustained then only by the scaling of precipitous cliffs overhanging the sea, 800 to 1,200 feet high, in order to snare the wild sea-birds which nested there in millions or to recover their eggs. If then a young man wished to marry and burden the small community with a family, he had to be put through a terrible ordeal. Taken to the highest point, overhanging the angriest sea, he had there to balance himself on his left foot on the outer edge of the cliff. That done, he had to extend the right foot into mid-air. that done, he had to throw out both arms, and if he returned to safety he was permitted to marry.

This seemed to me incredibly hard and even cruel until I heard from another young man, Eoghan Carmichael,[1] brought up with his parents in the Isle of Benbecula, that in his youth, long after the passing of the rock-balancing ordeal, he had noticed that the wee baby boys in the Isles no sooner accomplished the difficult task of balancing themselves and standing on their two legs than they began to practice—on a *low* rock— to balance on the left foot, right foot extended, so when it came to the day of the ordeal, it had been but an extension of a game they had played all their lives.

Men have been known to live in that rock isle to the age of ninety, who had all their lives scaled those perilous cliffs. Ever able they had been to swing their bodies to and fro, up or down, if they but got purchase in a cleft of the rock for the nail-joints of their fingers.

But not only in England and Scotland and across the Atlantic have we found enthusiasm for those Celtic songs. In 1927 we sang them in Amsterdam, The Hague, and Paris. This autumn, just as these pages go to press, we are preparing to visit Berlin, Prague, and Vienna. In Prague we have been chosen to represent Scotland in the League of Nations Folk-Art Congress.

Folk-song has come into its own of late years. The University of Edinburgh has set its mark on the place assigned to such racial lore by conferring on me the honorary degree of Doctor of Music.

Gaels have always been partial to threes. We published three volumes entitled *Songs of the Hebrides* with Messrs. Boosey and Company. These were to form a complete work. We published a fourth volume as a sort of appendix,[2] this time in Scotland, with Paterson's Publications. To differentiate it from the others it was entitled *From the Hebrides*. The head of the firm of Boosey kindly smiled, and remarked: 'It is time that Scotland was having a look-in.' When this fourth volume came out I had

[1] One of the sons of Dr. Alexander Carmichael. He received injuries in the war to which he finally succumbed. His little brochure on Celtic ornament is published by 'An Comun Gaidhealach'.
[2] Like Mary Macleod's 'Only a cronan'.

been over head and ears in the work for twenty years. There may or may not be another. The material is still accumulating.

Of the old singers to whose enthusiasm we owe the preservation of the songs to these days I would like here again to mention, in Eriskay: Gillespie McInnes's mother, who sang to me 'The Christ Child's Lullaby'; and Penny O'Henley, the 'Mermaid's Croon'. In Barra: Mrs. Macdonald, Skallary, who made a record (so faint you must hold your breath to hear it) of the 'Fairy Plaint'; Mrs. Maclean, Mrs. Cameron, Mrs. Boyd (from Mingulay), who sang to me 'Kishmul's Galley'; Ealasaid of the Glen, who sang me the airs of 'Fionn's Keening for Oscar' and 'The Sea-Feast'; Mrs. McKinnon, North Bay, who out of her rare musical memory has given me lavishly of her store; and lastly Kirsty McKinnon, Eigg; Lexie Macrae of South Harris; and Mary Ross of Kilmoluag, Skye.

Of the many young men and maidens who have contributed to this gathering of old Celtic melodies I can only say that without their share the work would have suffered great loss. We now hand it on to them in its written form with our thanks for the joy it has brought to us, remembering an old Gaelic saying:

A short giving with the gold—
A long giving with the song.

And now the work is done. But I hope still to carry on on the concert platform and shall probably never give a farewell recital. Since the day when, only twelve years old, I walked on holding my father's hand, I have been more at home on the concert platform than anywhere else. In recitals such as my father gave, and in which I try to follow him, you enter an ideal world and you take your audience with you. You lose your own individuality.

After she retired, Ellen Terry once said to me it was so boring now to be always Ellen Terry. In her stage life she had been so many interesting characters and had to be Ellen Terry for only a few hours a day. Now, she had to be Ellen Terry all day long. Some of us think that that could not be so very boring after all.

Of three things I am proud: that Ellen Terry, whom I have always adored, took me in her arms and kissed me after sitting through our London recitals with intense concentration; that Frances Tolmie, the ancient cultured Skye woman, the pioneer Hebridean song-collector whose memory I revere, raised her hands and blessed me and my work when last we parted in Dunvegan, Skye; that Ernest Newman, the philosopher-critic whose taste is so truly catholic and who came to a hearing of our work with no bias in its favour, gave it the highest praise.

Many another triolet I might add of the minds and characters that have influenced me: my father, the artist; my husband, the scientist; Matthay, the artist-scientist. Niecks, the historian; Wilfrid Gibson, the poet; Kenneth Macleod, the dreamer. Alexander Carmichael, who blazed the folk-lore trail in the Outer Isles; John Duncan, the Celtic painter, who found for me there the spot on which I could best begin work; and lastly Patrick Geddes, the pan-instigator, so to speak, who prodded us all into setting forth on the 'hill of difficulty'.

And if it has been sometimes a hard ascent, there has been invigorating fresh air at least and some joyful resting places in the Life of Song.

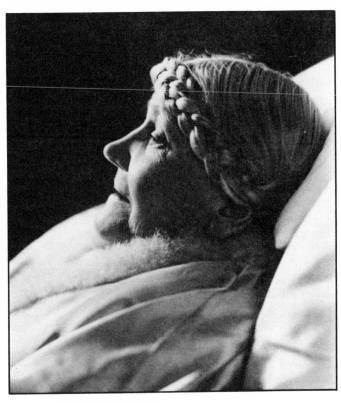

Marjory Kennedy-Fraser; her last official portrait.
(Courtesy of Mrs. Marjory Piggott).

171

Glossary

Au = Australian   C = Celtic   D = Dutch   E = English   F = French
G = Gaelic   I = Italian   Ir = Irish   L = Latin   L.S. = Lowland Scots
S.A. = South African

aff	off; away	L.S.
assegais	long spears	S.A.
au marché	to the market	F
au paradis	in paradise	F
awfu' dreich	awfully dull (or tedius)	L.S.
bairns	children	L.S.
Bean Shomhairle		
Bhig	Little Samuel's wife	G
bealach	pass	G
bel canto	Italian vocal style—18th century	I
birlinn	a 16-oared Celtic galley	C
Black House	type of highland dwelling	E
bodachan	little old man	G
brae	slope; hillside	L.S.
brava tosa	good (or brave) 'shorn one'	I
ca'	call	L.S.
cameriera	chambermaid	I
cavalieri serventi	gallant male escorts	I
"che belle		
gambe"	"what beautiful legs"	I
coup de glotte	blow of the glottis	I
crack	conversation	L.S.
cailleach	old woman	G
ceilidh	folk gathering with entertainment; concert	G
clachan	village	L.S.
Cuchullan	Irish folk hero	Ir

173

Dierdre	Celtic (Irish) heroine	I
duan	poem; ode; song	G
due scozzessi	two rascals	I
Dopper	Rigidly Calvanistic sect of Afrikaaners	S.A.
dry-stane	drystone	L.S.
élan	spring; dash; impetus	F
egregissimo	standing out from the crowd	I
faute de mieux	for want of something better	F
"Gaidhlig gu leor"	" 'plenty' Gaelic"	G.
gaed aff	went off	L.S.
Gaelic	Celtic language	G
glaur	mud; dirt	L.S.
ilk	of the same (family, class)	L.S.
keening	lamenting	Ir
kloof	ravine	S.A.
kirk	church	L.S.
kist	large chest	L.S.
kye	cows	L.S.
legato	connected	I
lochan	small loch or lake	L.S.
Machair	sandy dunes	G
maestro del canto	teacher of singing	I
"mais nous avons changetout cela"	"but we have changed all that"	F
oidhche mhath	good night	G
outspan	to unyolk; to unharness; encamp	S.A.

puirt a bial	mouth music	G
petit pains	small breads; buns	F
padrona	landlady; proprietress	I
pend	pen; enclosure	L.S.
petites gourmandes	little gluttons	F
prova generale	rehearsal	I
rara avis	rare bird; extraordinary	L
rubato	cheating on timing (musically)	I
salle	room	F
slancio	enthusiasm; impulse	I
snod	snug; tidy	E
sotto voce	soft; under one's breath	I
sostenuto	sustained	I
stoep	veranda	S.A.
swagsman (swagman)	tramp	Au
"suas leis an oran"	"up with the song"	G
trek	journey by ox wagon	S.A.
tutti	all together	I
villeggiatura	a holiday	I
waulking	process of fulling (cleansing and thickening)	G
wifie	dim. of wife	L.S.

Index

Aberdeen University 82, 103
Act of Touch, The 85
Aillte 149
Alan Glen's Technical School 82-3
Allan, Father 99, 101, 104, 105, 114, 144
America 13, 35-37, 153-156
Aoidh, Nic Iain 119, 120
Armstrong, Mrs. (Melba) 19, 71, 72
Art song 90-92, 106
Australia 16, 18, 19-27, 28, 35, 71, 72, 76

Ballad of MacNeill of Barra, The 119
Bantock, Branville 121, 157, 158, 159
Barra 116, 117, 118, 119, 120, 123, 124, 125, 141, 142, 144, 145, 146, 147, 162, 163, 164, 165
Barra Love Lilt 130
Barraich, Calum 148, 149, 150
Barrie, Sir James 14
Bauer, Frances Emilie 155
Benbecula 141, 148, 149, 150, 168
Benbecula Bridal 128
Ben Ledi, The 16, 17, 18
Bayreuth 87, 88
Birlinn of Clanranald, The 129, 130
Birlinn of The While Shoulders, The 128
Black House 103, 142-143

Blackie, Professor 70
Bonnie Prince Charlie 148
Boosey, Arthur 123
Boughton, Rutland 120, 121
Boyd, Mrs. 169
Boult, Sir Adrian 159
Breton 89, 90, 131
Burns, Robert 127

Cameron of Locheil 5
Cameron, Mrs. 169
Campbell, George S. 82, 154
Canada 35, 37, 38, 76, 77, 154
Cape, The (South Africa) 43, 44, 45, 46, 47, 48
Caristiona 127, 130, 161
Carmichael, Dr. Alexander 105, 110, 129, 143, 144, 148, 170
Carmichael, Eoghan 168
Carmina Gadelica 105, 110, 148
Ceilidh 89, 100, 103, 111, 112
Celtic, Celts 89, 91, 95, 98, 99, 105, 106, 108, 109, 110, 122, 123, 168
Charlie, Prince 100, 148
Chicago University 95
Christ Child's Lullaby, The 116, 133, 169
Churning Lilt, The 129
Civil List pension 141
Clanranald's Parting Song 120
Cockle Gatherer, The 166
Colum, Padraic 155
Common Sense in Singing 137
Corder, Frederick 84

Cornell University   153
Crone's Lilt, The   128
Crone's Creel, The   128–129

Dance to Your Shadow   166
David Kennedy, The Scots Singer   82
Davies, Ben   42
Death Croon, The   128, 130
Death Keening of a Hero   130
Deidre's Farewell   130
Ducoudray, Bourgault   89, 90, 100, 106, 118
Duhamel, M.   131
Duncan, John   95, 96, 105, 170

Ealasaid of the Glen   169
Edinburgh   41, 81, 82, 83, 84, 86, 105, 126, 139
Edinburgh Music Education Society   90
Edinburgh Evening News   105, 132
Edinburgh University   107, 168
Eigg   151, 152
Eriskay   18, 95, 96, 97, 98, 105, 107, 108, 109, 110, 114, 115
Eriskay Love Lilt, The   167
Eye of Springtide   166

Fairy Lull-song, The   161
Fairy Plaint, The   117, 169
Farr, Florence   138
Fionn's Keening for Oscar   169
Forbes-Robertson, John   39, 40, 60, 81
Fraser, Alec Yule   82, 83
Freer, Miss Goodrich   96
From the Hebrides   168

Gaelic   5, 11, 69, 70, 106, 128
Gambardella   56, 57, 58

Geddes, Patrick   89, 170
Gibson, Wilfrid   133, 170
Gillespie   100, 101, 111, 169
Glasgow   16, 83
Gow, Nathaniel   28
Gow, Neil   28
Graves, Alfred Perceval   123, 158
Gregory, Lady   138
Grierson, Professor   103

Harmsworth Educator, The 95, 103
Harris Love Lament, The   128
Harper, The   128
Hay, Jane   120
Heartling of My Heart   128
Hebrid Seas, In   121, 122
Hebridean Sea-Reivers, The 128
Henderson, Helen   6
Henderson, Robert   9
Herding Prayer   161
Hess, Myra   152
Hogmanay   143
Holbrooke, Joseph   158
Hull, Dr. Eaglefield   167

I Promessi Sposi   61
Immortal Hour, The   120, 121
Iona   141
Iona Rainbow, The   166
Islay Reaper, The   128
Island Sheiling Song   129
Italy   49–61, 62

Jackson, Sir Barry   157, 159
Johnson, Annie   124, 125, 128, 144, 145, 162
Johnson, Calum   131
Johnson, Patrick   22, 23, 26

Kelly Gang, The   21

Kelly, (Ned)   21
Kennedy, Charles (Marjory's
  brother)   37, 40, 42, 43, 66,
  91, 133, 139
Kennedy, David (Marjory's
  brother)   13, 26, 30, 36, 37,
  39, 40, 41, 55, 60
Kennedy, David Sr. (Marjory's
  father)   13, 14, 19, 23, 25,
  26, 28, 29, 32, 40, 41, 43, 46,
  60, 72, 74, 76, 77, 81
Kennedy, David (Marjory's son)
  83, 84, 107, 122
Kennedy, Elizabeth Fraser
  (Marjory's mother)   6, 24,
  32, 72, 81
Kennedy, Helen   13, 20, 22, 32,
  40, 43, 55, 60, 66, 69, 73, 76,
  81, 82
Kennedy, James   13, 40, 43,
  50, 51, 52, 53, 54, 59, 60, 62,
  63, 64, 65
Kennedy, Jessie   76, 84, 85, 89,
  137, 141, 144, 151, 152
Kennedy, John (Marjory's
  brother)   14, 91, 137, 151
Kennedy, Kate   40, 43, 62, 63,
  64, 65
Kennedy, Lizzie   40, 41, 43, 46,
  55, 62, 63, 64, 65
Kennedy, Margaret   14, 57, 69,
  73, 76, 81, 84, 87, 91, 123,
  137, 151, 153, 160, 161
Kennedy, Patuffa   83, 84, 107,
  108, 111, 112, 113, 116, 118,
  122, 132, 133, 141, 144, 153,
  154, 155, 156, 157, 158, 160
Kennedy, Robert   25, 40, 43,
  49, 50, 51, 52, 53, 59, 65, 66,
  71, 76
Kishmul's Galley   118, 119,
  125, 128, 137, 169

Krehbiel   154

La Donadio   64
Lamperti   41, 56, 59, 62, 63, 65
Land, Edward   8
Land of Heart's Desire   129
League of Nations Folk Art
  Congress   168
Leaping Galley   161
Lerwick   10, 11
Leverhulme, Lord   23, 160
Lewes, The   160, 161
Lewis   23
Lindsay, Lady Kathleen   160
Logan, Mrs.   69
London   7, 9, 15, 39, 76, 137,
  138, 157
Lord of the Isles, The   128
Love Wandering   138

MacDonald, Alexander   129
Macdonald, Flora   148, 161
MacDonald, Mrs. (Skallary
  169
Macdonald, Peggy   110
MacDowell Society of New
  York 153
Macinnes, Duncan   102, 107
Mackellar, Mary   70
Mackenzie, Sir Alexander   84
Mackenzie, Sir Leslie   142
Maclean, Mrs. Joseph   116, 123
Macleod, Fiona (William Sharp)
  121
Macleod, Janet   151
Macleod, Kenneth   42, 107, 123,
  126–133, 151, 152, 166, 170
Macleod, Mary   129, 130
Macleod, Marion   166
Macleod (of Skeabost)   161
MacMillan, Dugald   99
MacMillan, Mairi Mhor   99

Macneill, Annie 112
Macneill, Ishbel 144
Macneill, Rev. John 112, 114,
  116, 118, 119
Macneill, Michael 118, 119
Macpherson (Ossian) 148
Macphie, Hector 120
Macrae, Lexie 161, 169
Marchesi, Mathilde 57, 58, 66,
  67, 68, 69, 72, 86
Marchesi, Blanche 66
Masters, Lee 155
Matthay School 107, 122, 132
Matthay, Tobias 84–85, 86,
  103, 137, 152, 170
MacInnes, Gillespie 100, 101,
  111, 169
MacInnes, John 103, 116
MacInnes, Mary 96
McKinnon, Kirsty 169
McKinnon, Mrs. (North Bay)
  125, 162, 169
McKinnon, Professor 126
Melba 19, 71, 72
Mermaid's Croon, The 114,
  115, 169
Milking Croon 129
Moody, Mrs. Vaughn 155
Mull Fisher's Song, The 100,
  107, 129
Munro, Hon. James 22, 71

New Zealand 16, 29, 32, 33,
  34, 71, 72–75
Newman, Ernest 130, 157, 170
Nice 62–65
Niecks, Frederick 87, 90, 91,
  170

O'Henley, Penny 111, 114,
  115, 169
Old Crone's Lilt, The 53

Ossian (James Macpherson) 148
Ossian's Midsummer Dream
  129

Packard, Mrs. 28
Pan-Celtic Congress 123
Patie Birnie 41
Perth 6, 8, 9
Potato-lifting, The 128
Princeton University 153
Punch 164
Putting Out to Sea 166
Paris 66

Queen Victoria 9

Reade, Ernest 151
Renan 98, 108
Repetto 63
Rhys, Ernest 123
Ricordi 137
Righini 51, 52
Ristori 58
Road to the Isles, The 131
Ross, Mary 161, 169
Rune of the Weaver, The 166
San Giovanni 41, 56, 86
Sandberg, Carl 155
Scholes, Percy 121
Scott, Cyril 158
Sea Feast 130, 169
Sea Longing 128
Sea Moods 130
Sea Procession 130
Sea Quest 130
Sea Sorrow 128
Sea Sounds 128
Sea Tangle 130–131
Seabird Flying Hither, Tell Me
  166
Seagull of the Land-under-
  Waves, The 128, 158, 161

Seal Maiden, The 130
Seal Woman's Sea Joy 163
Seal-Woman, The 158
Sharp, Mrs. William 123
Shelving, Paul 159
Skye Fisher's Song, The 100, 107, 129
Sleeps the Noon in the Deep Blue Sky 129
Songs of the Hebrides 137, 168
South Africa (The Cape) 43, 44, 46–48, 83
South African Farm 61
Spinning Song 130
St. Abb's Haven 120, 121
St. Kilda 20, 167
Summer Meeting 89, 95, 106

Taylor, Rachel Annand 103
Terry, Ellen 53, 153, 169, 170
Théâtre des Italiens 64, 65
Thomson, Arthur 89
To the Isle of Skye 161
To People Who Have Gardens 166

To the Sea King of the Isles 130
Tolmie, Frances 114, 161, 170

Valenti 51, 52, 53
Vogrich, Max 71

voice production 41, 42, 56–59, 60, 62, 63, 66, 67, 68, 69

Waddell, Maimie 163
Waddell, Ruth 162, 163
Watson, Mrs. E. C. 129
waulking songs 110, 145–147, 164, 165
Weaving Lilt, The 128
Wind on the Moor 166
Wilson, John 40
Wordsworth 108, 109

Yeats, W. B. 109, 138
Yont the Coolins 161